ALLEN CARR'S
EASY WAY
TO QUIT
EMOTIONAL
EATING

Request · Read · Return

...Your Library. Delivered.

This item was purchased for the Library through Zip Books, a statewide project of the NorthNet Library System, funded by the California State Library.

ALLEN CARR'S
EASY WAY
TO QUIT
EMOTIONAL
EATING

SIRIUS

To the former emotional eaters all over the world who can testify personally to the effectiveness of Allen Carr's Easyway method and without whom this book would not have been possible

Thanks also to Tim Glynne-Jones for additional editorial input

SIRIUS

This edition published in 2021 by Sirius Publishing, a division of Arcturus Publishing Limited,
26/27 Bickels Yard, 151–153 Bermondsey Street,
London SE1 3HA

ISBN: 978-1-78950-004-2
AD005773US

Printed in the USA

This book is not intended to take the place
of advice from a trained medical professional

ALLEN CARR

Allen Carr was a chain-smoker for over 30 years. In 1983, after countless failed attempts to quit, he went from 60–100 cigarettes a day to zero without suffering withdrawal pangs, without using willpower, and without putting on weight. He realized that he had discovered what the world had been waiting for—the easy way to stop smoking—and embarked on a mission to help cure the world's smokers.

As a result of the phenomenal success of his method, he gained an international reputation as the world's leading expert on quitting smoking and his network of centers now spans the globe. His first book, *Allen Carr's Easy Way to Stop Smoking*, has sold over 14 million copies, remains a global bestseller, and has been published in more than 40 different languages. Hundreds of thousands of smokers have successfully quit at Allen Carr's Easyway centers where they guarantee you'll find it easy to stop or your money back.

Allen Carr's brilliant Easyway method has been successfully applied to weight control, alcohol, debt, refined sugar, and a host of other addictions and issues.

For more information about Allen Carr's Easyway, please
visit **www.allencarr.com**

Allen Carr's Easyway

The key that will set you free

CONTENTS

INTRODUCTION

BY JOHN DICEY, GLOBAL CEO & SENIOR THERAPIST,
ALLEN CARR'S EASYWAY

- Do you reward yourself with food?

- Do you eat to comfort yourself or feel secure? Or do you restrict what you eat to feel in control?

- Does your eating increase when you're stressed or sad?

- Do you keep eating even when you're full?

- Do you avoid food altogether sometimes or often?

- Do you engage in frequent or occasional binge-eating?

- Do you ever wish you could resist the urge to eat? Or find it difficult to bring yourself to eat?

- Have you ever purged food (this includes self-induced vomiting, misuse of laxatives, diuretics, or enemas), or has the thought of purging food ever crossed your mind?

- Do you feel controlled by food?

If you answered yes to any of the above, it's an indication that your relationship with food is causing you stress and pressure. Negative emotions are interfering with your appetite and digestion process in a dysfunctional and distorted way.

However, this book doesn't intend to get bogged down with medical or psychological labels. All the symptoms listed in the questions on the previous page can be factors in a whole host of diagnosable conditions.

These range from "Emotional Eating" (often labeled as "Emotional Overeating") to issues considered to be far more serious, such as "Other Specified Feeding or Eating Disorder" (OSFED), "Binge Eating Disorder", "Bulimia," and "Anorexia".

These latter conditions are all serious mental illnesses. They can affect anyone of any age, gender, or background. If you feel or fear that you might be suffering from any of these more serious conditions, then please consult your family doctor. It's natural to feel nervous about sharing any worries you may have, but it's really important that you do so.

If you need a little help to get to that stage, there are plenty of amazing charities and organizations out there who will lend you an anonymous ear in a kind, gentle, understanding, knowledgeable, and non-judgmental way. The value of just speaking to someone is incalculable.

This book doesn't pretend to take the place of the kind of help and support that you may need from your doctor and medical advisors in the event that you have a condition such as Binge Eating Disorder, Bulimia, or Anorexia, but there is no reason why it shouldn't help you to establish a healthier understanding of your relationship with food and your emotions.

Whichever category you fall into, there is nothing within these pages that might cause you any harm or hindrance, and much that might help you unlock the prison door that keeps you in the emotional eating trap.

Emotional eating is defined as using food to attempt to relieve negative emotions, rather than to relieve hunger. It leads to a complex and unhappy relationship with food, a tendency to overeat and put on weight, accompanied by feelings of helplessness, sluggishness, and self-loathing. You may have tried and failed to control your eating by dieting or just willing yourself to stop. What you need is a method that truly understands the multiple psychological, rather than the physical, causes of emotional eating and how to untangle them.

"WHAT ON EARTH CAN A CURE FOR SMOKING OFFER ME?"

That's a good question. Twenty or so years ago, I had a serious problem. I was addicted to cigarettes. Not only that, I smoked 80 a day and had given up all hope of ever being able to quit. I had no idea that the cause of my condition was almost entirely psychological—as was the solution. I wasn't happy that I smoked, but I believed it was my fate and all attempts to convince me otherwise were completely pointless.

I was fortunate. I had a wife who wasn't prepared to give in so easily. Under duress, I agreed to attend Allen Carr's center in London, on the understanding that when I walked out, still a confirmed smoker, she would allow me to smoke in peace, without hassling me about it, for at least 12 months.

No one was more surprised than I was, or perhaps my wife, that I walked out of that seminar convinced that I would never smoke again.

If I had been more open-minded, it would not have surprised me. By the time I went along, Allen had already helped millions of people to quit through his live seminar centers and books. The evidence was plain to see, but, being a chain-smoker whose entire existence revolved around "the next cigarette," I couldn't see it.

In hindsight, I can say that part of me didn't want to see it. It took my own life-changing experience to convince me. Little did I know back then that two decades later Allen Carr's brilliant method would also save me from Type 2 diabetes by curing my lifelong addiction to "bad carbs."

ALLEN CARR'S EASYWAY METHOD IS TRULY LIFE-CHANGING

For a third of a century, Allen himself had chain-smoked 60 to 100 cigarettes a day. With the exception of acupuncture, he had tried all the conventional and unconventional methods to quit. Eventually, like me, he gave up even trying to quit, believing "once a smoker, always a smoker," and resigned himself to a premature death. Then he made a discovery that inspired him to try again.

As he described it, "I went overnight from 100 cigarettes a day to zero—without any bad temper or sense of loss, void, or depression. On the contrary, I actually enjoyed the process. I knew I was already a nonsmoker even before I had extinguished my final cigarette and I've never had the slightest urge to smoke since."

It was a revelation to Allen, who realized that he had discovered a method that would enable any smoker to quit:

• Easily, immediately, and painlessly

• Without using willpower, aids, substitutes, or gimmicks

• Without suffering depression or withdrawal symptoms

• Without gaining weight

After using his smoking friends and relatives as guinea pigs, he gave up his lucrative profession as a qualified accountant and set up a clinic to help other smokers to quit. He gave his method its name, EASYWAY, and so successful has it been that there are now Allen Carr's Easyway centers in more than 150 cities in 50 countries worldwide. Bestselling books based on his method are now translated into over 40 languages, with more being added each year.

It quickly became clear to Allen that his method could be applied to any addictive drug or behavioral issue, not just nicotine. The method has now helped tens of millions of people to quit smoking, alcohol .and illicit drugs, and to tackle sugar and carb addiction, weight issues, gambling, overspending, fear of flying, and digital/tech addiction.

I was so inspired by Allen and what I saw as his miraculous method that I hassled and harangued him and Robin Hayley (now chairman of Allen Carr's Easyway) to let me get involved in their quest to cure the world of smoking.

To my good fortune, I succeeded in convincing them. Being trained by Allen and Robin was one of the most rewarding experiences of my life. To be able to count Allen as not only my coach and mentor but also my friend was an amazing honor and privilege.

SHARING THE TRUTH

Over the past 20 years, I have gone on to treat more than 30,000 smokers myself at Allen's original London center and lead the team that has taken his method from Berlin to Bogota, New Zealand to New York, Sydney to Santiago. Tasked by Allen with insuring that his legacy achieves its full potential, we've taken Allen Carr's Easyway from videos to DVD, from clinics to apps, from computer games to audio books, to online programs, video-on-demand, and beyond.

Behind this phenomenal success lies one simple truth—a truth that Allen discovered by chance and passed on to tens of millions of people like me. What connects us all is that none of us expected to be changed in the way we were. We were all skeptical, all laboring under the same illusions.

The truth about compulsive behaviors like smoking and emotional eating is kept hidden from most of us by a carefully orchestrated campaign of cover-ups and falsehoods. We live in a world ruled by fictions of every kind. We are manipulated from all sides by organizations and individuals that claim to be helping us but are really more interested in our money; we are constantly bombarded by messages from the advertising industry.

There are traps set to snare us by conning us into doing things that we know are bad for us with misinformation about "fun" and "individuality" and "freedom of choice." That's why some people who manage to quit addictions and behaviors by using willpower still go on feeling the cravings, sometimes for the rest of their lives. They never shake off the belief that they are making a sacrifice, "giving up" something that provides them with pleasure or comfort, or makes them more fun and sociable.

Understanding the simple truth and recognizing how it applies to you is the key to escaping the trap of emotional eating, and more importantly, staying free from its problems permanently.

This book will help you to see the simple truth. It is not a diet book. It doesn't rely on guilt, bullying, or scare tactics. As you will learn, all those techniques actually make it harder to quit. Instead, it gives you a structured, easy-to-follow method for overcoming your emotional eating problem quickly, painlessly, and permanently. This book has been written with the active cooperation of former emotional eaters from all over the world who can testify personally to the effectiveness of Allen Carr's Easyway.

ALLEN'S VOICE

The responsibility for insuring our books are faithful to Allen Carr's original method is mine. It has been suggested to me that I describe myself as the author of the books we've published since Allen passed away. In my view that would be quite wrong.

That's because every new book is written strictly in accordance with Allen Carr's brilliant Easyway method. In our new books, we have merely updated and amended the format to bring it up to date and make it as relevant as possible for the modern-day audience. There is not a word in our books that Allen didn't write or wouldn't have written if he was still with us and, for that reason, the updates, anecdotes, and analogies that are not his own work—that were contemporized or added by me—are written clearly in Allen's voice to seamlessly complement the original text and method.

I consider myself privileged to have worked so closely with Allen on Easyway books while he was alive, gaining insight into how the method could be applied, and exploring and mapping out its future evolution. I was more than happy to have the responsibility for continuing this vital mission placed on my shoulders by Allen himself. It's a responsibility I accepted with humility and one I take extremely seriously.

Not only did Allen Carr free me from an addiction to nicotine that would otherwise have killed me years ago, he taught me everything I know about the mental processes that put me in that predicament and how to unravel them easily, painlessly, and without the need for willpower.

Having worked on Allen's books for nearly 20 years, I still take pleasure in deflecting all the praise and acclaim straight back to the great man himself: It's all down to Allen Carr.

The method is as pure, as bright, as adaptable, and as effective as it's ever been, allowing us to apply it to a whole host of problems aside from smoking. Whether it's overeating or alcoholism, gambling, or junk spending, fear of flying, mindfulness, or even "hard" drugs, the method guides those who need help in a simple, relatable, plain-speaking way.

I know from happy experience that the benefits of following this method can be life-changing. So let me pass you into the safest of hands —Allen Carr and his Easyway.

John Dicey
Global CEO & Senior Therapist, Allen Carr's Easyway

Chapter 1

THE KEY

Has eating ceased to be a pleasure for you? Do you feel trapped by food? Do you find yourself helpless to resist the temptation of junk food, even when you're not hungry? It's time to escape the miserable prison of emotional eating and the good news is, you're holding the key.

Emotional eating is a disorder that involves the use of food in an attempt to relieve uncomfortable emotions, such as anxiety, stress, loneliness, and boredom. Most people have experienced the compulsion to "comfort eat" when feeling low, bored, or under pressure, but that compulsion can take over your life, causing a destructive cycle of eating, guilt, misery… and more eating.

A BOLD CLAIM

This book is for people who have found themselves caught up in this vicious circle. It is not a diet book. Diets don't work. They focus too much on physical appearance and neglect what's going on in the mind.

This is why dieting always feels like hard work—even if you reach your target, you abandon the diet and start piling on the pounds again.

This book tackles the psychological process that leads to emotional eating. It will help you to understand what's going on in your mind and why, and then help you to change your mindset so that you no longer feel inclined to comfort eat.

Unlike dieting, you won't have to make any sacrifices. You won't have to draw on all your willpower to overcome a feeling of deprivation. You will find that, having conquered your issues with emotional eating, you won't be susceptible to falling back into the trap.

Perhaps you find this claim a little too good to be true. Conventional wisdom tells us that problems like emotional eating are complex and require immense willpower to overcome. This book will show you that conventional wisdom is misguided. Not only that, it is actually counterproductive when it comes to curing addictive conditions like emotional eating.

The truth is that you have the power to overcome emotional eating without any pain or sacrifice, regardless of who you are or what your personal circumstances may be. All you need is an open mind.

If you're skeptical about that, ask yourself one question: Has conventional wisdom worked for you until now? If it had, you wouldn't be reading this book.

THE "A" WORD

The complexity with emotional eating is that it has nothing to do with genuine hunger. Emotional eating is not a compulsion to eat nutritious foods, like fruit and vegetables; it demands foods that deliver a quick hit of what we've come to perceive as "pleasure" or "comfort": sugary foods, starchy carbs, and salty foods. These foods have little or no nutritional value. Unfortunately, they're also highly addictive. Another good word for them is "junk," and the reason we turn to these foods has nothing to do with genuine pleasure or comfort and everything to do with addiction.

Throughout this book I will use the terms "junk" and "junk food" to include all the nonnutritious, addictive foods that emotional eaters use, such as candy, cakes, cookies, chocolate, potato chips, bread, and fast food. These foods are junk because they fill the stomach without giving your body the nutrients it needs. For reasons I will explain later in the book, the craving for them doesn't stop even when your stomach is full. Understanding that can be quite a revelation; it perfectly explains why someone who eats these foods persistently overeats.

We tend to make light of our desire for these "comfort foods" by jokingly claiming to being addicted.

"I'm a chocaholic."

"I'm a carb addict."

"I have a sugar addiction."

But it doesn't really occur to anyone that emotional eating genuinely is a form of addiction. Addictions take hold when a part of the brain known colloquially as the "reward pathways" comes into play.

By making us feel good when we do something that is healthy or beneficial for us, the reward pathways encourage us to keep doing those things.

But drugs like heroin and nicotine hijack the reward pathways and have them behave dysfunctionally, causing us to confuse genuine pleasures with phoney ones.

The phoney pleasures are always followed by a big low. That's the difference between genuine pleasures and the false pleasures we get from drugs: Genuine pleasures give you a lasting high and don't leave you feeling low or guilty afterward. It's not just the obvious drugs that hijack the reward pathways—sugar and "bad carbs" do exactly the same.

If your favorite foods tend to be bread, pasta, rice, or potato-based, not of course forgetting refined sugar (desserts, chocolate, cakes, and pastries, etc.), then it's likely that you suffer from an addiction to "bad carbs." My book *Good Sugar Bad Sugar* contains a lot more about that and you might find that beneficial once you've tackled the issue of emotional eating. I promise not to go into too much detail about addiction to other drugs such as nicotine or heroin, but at times it will be useful to refer to them to illustrate a point.

When the phoney boost from a drug (or junk food) wears off, you are left with a restless, empty feeling. In addiction terms, we call this withdrawal. When you take a second shot of the drug, the slight discomfort of withdrawal is relieved. We instantly feel better. But the withdrawal feeling returns, empty and restless. Your brain remembers that the second shot of the drug seemed to relieve the discomfort caused by the withdrawal from the first shot of the drug.

The brain is therefore conned into seeing the drug as pleasurable—relief from withdrawal begins to masquerade as a pleasure or reward. The brain therefore starts to trigger cravings for more of the drug as the withdrawal feeling kicks in again.

The removal of the discomfort caused by the withdrawal simply enables the addict to feel momentarily normal again. In other words, the addict takes the next shot of the drug to feel like someone who isn't addicted to the drug. This confidence trick is the basis of all drug addiction.

It's actually an ingenious process, which twists reality and traps you in a tangle of illusions. But when you see through the illusions—as you will—it all becomes incredibly clear. Addicts always crave bigger and bigger doses as the phoney pleasure diminishes.

PHONEY PLEASURE DIMINISHING = WITHDRAWAL FROM THE DRUG

WITHDRAWAL FROM THE DRUG WAS CAUSED
BY THE FIRST SHOT OF THE DRUG

A SHOT OF THE DRUG DOESN'T END THE WITHDRAWAL
—IT PARTIALLY RELIEVES IT BEFORE CREATING
THE NEXT BOUT OF WITHDRAWAL

Like all addicts, chronic emotional eaters complain of deriving no pleasure from the foods they binge on, yet feel powerless to stop eating them—in spite of the guilt and self-loathing it inflicts . This is a classic symptom of addiction: A choice intended to relieve emotional suffering ends up causing more of it.

It begins small, seemingly under control, but soon grows to the point where it takes you over and starts to destroy your life. You find yourself eating more and more junk, trying to get some satisfaction, but that never arrives. Feeling unable to stop eating junk despite the harm you know it's causing you is another sure sign of addiction.

As with all addictions, it's the illusion that the behavior provides a genuine pleasure or comfort that keeps you trapped. Smokers suffer the illusion that cigarettes help them relax. In fact, they do the complete opposite. The same misconceptions are at work when it comes to emotional eating. Foods that you regard as a treat actually make you miserable. Yet the illusion of pleasure remains.

It's a vicious circle and the longer you go on laboring under the illusion that eating junk gives you pleasure or comfort, the more miserable you become.

There is a tendency for parents to pass emotional-eating behaviors on to their children too, either overfeeding them with junk or underfeeding them to compensate for their inability to control their own eating. Either way, an eating disorder can be passed on to the next generation, accompanied by the inevitable sense of guilt.

THE SIMPLE TRUTH

The term "emotional eating" implies that there is an underlying emotional problem that drives you to eat. It could be stress, depression, fear, heartbreak, a feeling of worthlessness, loneliness, boredom… or a combination of all these emotions. Whatever the cause, you won't arrive at the solution through eating. You've probably worked that out for yourself, yet you still can't seem to escape. The temptation to eat whenever you feel an emotional need is too great. It's as if you're being pinned down by a powerful monster.

The purpose of this book is to help you kill that monster and make the escape you know you need to make from the miserable, repetitive cycle of emotional eating. Without the tyranny of that monster, you can then deal with your emotions with a clear mind.

If the solution is as simple as I'm making out, you may be wondering why you haven't been able to see it for yourself.

That monster is quite ingenious. It wraps you up in confusion, yet the truth is incredibly simple…

THE ONLY WAY TO QUIT AN ADDICTION IS TO STOP DOING IT

Of course, there is more to Easyway than knowing this simple truth, but it's much more straightforward than other methods, which lose sight of the obvious: "The only way to quit an addiction is to stop doing it." It's *how* you go about stopping that matters.

There is nothing unusual about turning to food for comfort. The satisfaction of eating is hardwired into our DNA as part of our survival instinct. Everybody knows the temptation to eat too many cakes, chocolate, candy, and other things that aren't "good for you," and how that temptation ramps up when you're feeling stressed or sad. And because emotional eating involves a similar process to hunger eating, it's easy to confuse the two.

But they are NOT the same, and it's only when you find yourself caught up in the cycle of emotional eating that you realize how important the difference is. When you begin to comfort eat, you believe you are in control. You know that sugary and carb-laden foods are not "good for you," but feel sure that as long as you keep them in moderation it won't be a problem.

And there probably would be no harm if we *were* in control. We would be able to stop whenever we wanted to. But that's not the case, is it? The compulsion to eat junk grows, moderation flies out of the window, and the guilt and self-loathing flood in.

It's obvious that it's not the food itself that keeps you eating; there's something else, like an unseen force compelling you to do it. It's the same for all addictions. When you start to comfort eat, you believe you are in control and can keep it in moderation. But the more you eat for comfort, the more you lose control.

It's safe to assume from the fact that you're reading this book that you do not feel in control. Perhaps you've tried to address the eating problem in the past and found you couldn't. No matter how hard you tried, you lacked the willpower. Now you comfort eat even when you don't want to and you're powerless to stop.

This book will show you two very important truths:

YOU ARE NOT POWERLESS AND YOU DO NOT LACK WILLPOWER

THE REASON YOU HAVE FAILED TO OVERCOME EMOTIONAL EATING IN THE PAST IS SIMPLY BECAUSE YOU WERE FOLLOWING THE WRONG METHOD

IT'S TIME WE TALKED

Nobody likes to admit they've lost control. We regard self-control as a cornerstone of civilized behavior. It goes hand in hand with morality, dignity, and courtesy. Loss of control causes feelings of shame and thus problems like addiction and emotional eating are swept under the carpet. The person with the problem denies it; the rest try to avoid it.

KEEPING IT ALL TO YOURSELF CREATES A BURDEN THAT ONLY MAKES IT HARDER TO ESCAPE FROM THE TRAP

This is no way to tackle a problem. It makes you feel very alone and compels you to try to conceal it—from others and from yourself. Secretive behaviour creates even greater feelings of guilt and shame that deepen your misery.

The first necessity when tackling a problem like emotional eating is to acknowledge that you have it—or that it has you. The fact that you have picked up this book is a good sign that you've made that vital step. The next step is to do something about it.

The solution is in your hands. More accurately, it's in your mind. You need to break the cycle of misery and comfort eating. As you read through this book, be honest about your emotional eating and be prepared to open your mind to some truths that may seem hard to accept.

You are not alone—far from it. Emotional eating is a global problem, threatening the health and happiness of millions if not billions of people. As you open your mind to the truths contained in this book, this will become obvious to you.

It will also become apparent that your problem is not down to some failing in your personality. The more you allow yourself to open up and unravel these myths, the more you will understand that you can conquer your emotional eating. And you can do so without willpower.

A METHOD THAT WORKS

Easyway is a tried and tested way of escaping from addictive traps like emotional eating. It is built on the realization that addiction hijacks our instincts, so that the "fix" we turn to for relief is actually the "poison" that caused our problem in the first place.

That was the revelation that triggered this method. I was a confirmed nicotine addict, choking my way through 60 to 100 cigarettes a day and resigned to a premature death. I was under the misapprehension that smoking was a habit I had acquired and lacked the willpower to kick. The moment of revelation came when I realized that smoking wasn't just a habit: It was an addiction.

In that moment I saw with extraordinary clarity that my inability to quit smoking was neither a weakness in my character, nor some magical quality in the cigarette. It was the addiction, fooling me into seeking relief in the very thing that was causing my misery.

This led naturally to two indisputable conclusions:

• Smoking provides no genuine pleasure or comfort

• Therefore, stopping involves no sacrifice or deprivation

I quit there and then and never felt the temptation to smoke again.

I gave the method its name, Easyway, because it required no willpower, no substitutes, no gimmicks.

It simply enabled smokers to become happy nonsmokers by unraveling the brainwashing that convinced them that smoking was a pleasure or a comfort.

The method is still hugely successful in helping smokers all around the world to quit. Once they remove the illusion that they are making a sacrifice by stopping, they find it easy to quit because they don't feel deprived and they are happy to be free.

I realized that this method would work for all addictions and went on to apply it successfully to alcohol, other drugs, and even "drugless" addictions like gambling and digital/technology addiction.

The key was that all addictions are mainly a condition of the mind. With most drugs, the physical element is 1 percent; the mental element 99 percent. With behavioural addictions such as gambling, the physical element is also 1 percent and the mental element is 99 percent.

Easyway is about unraveling the misconceptions that drive you to do something that does you harm in the belief that it will give you pleasure. The principle applies to emotional eating, a discomfiting combination of physical and behavioral elements, just as it does to any other addiction or compulsive behavior.

WHAT THIS BOOK WILL DO FOR YOU

The aims of this book are to:

- Change the way you think about food

- Help you learn to eat mindfully and make food a pleasure again

- Show you how to put a stop to emotional eating—immediately, easily, and painlessly

- Enable you to be the weight you want to be

- Let you take control of your life again

It comes with several assurances: You won't be talked down to; you won't be subjected to scare tactics or gimmicks; you won't feel deprived; and by the end, you won't miss emotional eating.

By explaining how the addiction trap works and setting out simple, step-by-step instructions to help you get free, this book will show you how to approach eating for a healthier, happier life.

It will address the feeling of panic that can set in and cloud your judgment when trying to overcome addiction. It will help you to replace deceit, guilt, and shame with openness, honesty, and confidence; it will help you take control where you feel helpless; and it will replace misery with happiness.

There is no need for you to be miserable. You are not "giving up" anything.

Nothing bad is going to happen. You will not miss or yearn for anything. You will not feel there is a gap in your life.

On the contrary, your life will feel more complete, more balanced, and more relaxed.

THE INSTRUCTIONS

As you read through the book, you will come across a series of instructions. If you miss one of these instructions or fail to follow any of them, the method will not work. If you try to skip ahead and read the book in a different order from which it was written in, the method will not work.

Easyway is the key to freeing yourself from the trap you're in, and it works like the combination to unlock a safe: If you don't apply all the numbers in the correct order, the lock will not open.

As well as these instructions, I ask you not to make any changes to your eating at this stage. By the end of the book you will have a completely different attitude, but right now any attempt to change your diet will cause a distraction that we don't want. It's important that you're able to focus on the instructions in the book without any distractions.

FIRST INSTRUCTION:
FOLLOW ALL THE INSTRUCTIONS

Chapter 2

A WORLD OF TEMPTATION

IN THIS CHAPTER

• *OUR LOVE–HATE RELATIONSHIP WITH FOOD* • *THE BENEFITS OF JUNK FOOD*
• *THE ILLUSION OF PLEASURE* • *HOW CAN I STOP EATING?*

So how did this love–hate relationship with food start? Let's begin the conversation by taking a look at the way we eat today and the effect it is having on the human population.

Eating should be a pleasure. Human beings, like all animals, have been designed to enjoy food. We've been given a set of senses to help us identify when something is good to eat: If it looks good, smells good, and feels good, the chances are it will taste good too.

The pleasure we take in food isn't just a perk; it serves a vital purpose within our survival mechanism. By making good food attractive to our senses and bad food repulsive, our survival mechanism has given us a simple tool to protect us from eating anything harmful. All we have to do is follow our instincts, make sure we enjoy our food, and everything should be fine.

The same principle applies throughout the animal kingdom. Animals use their senses to select their food and avoid poisons. They will sniff it, prod it, and lick it before committing to eating it. They are giving their senses a chance to register "good" or "bad."

We have another tool that tells us when to eat and when to stop eating: Hunger. We are designed to feel hungry when our nutrient levels are running low and to feel satisfied when we've topped them up. Again, this is an instinct shared by all other animals.

When you look at animals in the wild, they always look fit, don't they? They don't appear to have issues with food, weight, and body image. A pack of wolves, a pride of lions, a herd of buffalo, a flock of birds, a school of fish… there is a uniformity in their body shape. You don't see overweight ones that struggle to keep up with the rest and are ashamed to go out because they can't help overeating. Even species that appear overweight, hippos, walruses, etc., are exactly the same shape and perfectly designed for their environment.

OUR LOVE-HATE RELATIONSHIP WITH FOOD

So why has this become a feature among humans? Where have we gone wrong?

The problem lies in the one thing that sets us apart from the rest of the animal kingdom: Intellect. We're cleverer than they are and we think we know better—better even than our own instincts. So when we're presented with the choice of an apple or a cake, we choose the cake because we think it will give us more pleasure.

Most animals wouldn't choose the cake. They would choose the apple. An apple is more colorful; it smells fresh and juicy; it feels firm and ripe. It checks all the boxes that instinctively tell an animal that it contains the nutrients it needs.

The cake is brown. It has very little aroma. It feels soft and crumbly. Most animals would turn their nose up at it. There are two main exceptions to that rule. First, domesticated animals, pets, whose diets we control and subsequently corrupt in the same way as we corrupt our own, and second wild animals who (literally) grow fat as a result of eating our food waste that mainly comprises highly addictive junk.

So why do we choose the cake?

Choosing junk food is an intellectual process. That doesn't mean it's clever; it just means it's a decision you make based on acquired knowledge rather than instinct. Next time you're tempted by a cake, cookie, potato chips, or other "comfort" food, test it out on your senses.

- How does it look?

- How does it smell?

- How does it feel?

Try to focus on each sense individually. When smelling and feeling it, close your eyes. You'll find there is very little to excite the senses. Any synthetic sugariness is acquired as a pavlovian response to our sugar addiction.

If we based our eating choices on our senses alone, we wouldn't eat junk food. So why do we eat it at all? These are the arguments commonly put forward in favor of junk food:

It's fast
It's convenient
It's cheap
It tastes great

These arguments are enough to convince us to eat junk food, even though we know it's not good for us. The lack of nutritional value doesn't bother us: We can make up for that with the next meal. Similarly, the known health risks of eating an excess of refined sugar and salt don't stop us: As long as we keep it in moderation we'll be all right.

Right?

The fact that you're reading this book indicates that all is not right. And there is plenty of evidence that you're not the only one. The world is in the grip of an obesity epidemic. That's a fact. According to the World Health Organization (WHO), worldwide obesity figures have almost trebled since 1975. Two in every five adults aged 18 or over are overweight; more than one in eight are obese. And we are passing the problem on to our children in even greater numbers.

FOR MORE THAN 2 BILLION PEOPLE ON THE PLANET, MODERATION HAS GONE OUT OF THE WINDOW

Another global health epidemic is Type 2 diabetes, once known as "adult onset diabetes" because, unlike Type 1, it usually comes on later in life and is mainly caused by poor diet and lack of exercise. Today, Type 2 diabetes is becoming more and more prevalent among younger people too. The total number of people with diabetes has quadrupled since 1980 and over 90 percent of cases are Type 2. The World Health Organization predicts that diabetes will be the seventh-leading cause of death by 2030.

OUR HIGH-SUGAR, HIGH-CARB DIET IS LITERALLY KILLING US

So why do we do it? Let's look more closely at those four arguments in favor of junk food.

THE BENEFITS OF JUNK FOOD

1. It's fast

The pace of life seems to increase year on year. We have less time for everything, so there is pressure to do it all in a hurry. We drive too fast, get impatient in lines, shout at our computers when they run a little slow… Within all this frenzy, we have to eat from time to time, so aren't we lucky that those clever people have come up with the perfect solution: Fast food!

With fast food, we don't have to break stride; we can eat on the go. Every second is precious, so the less time we have to spend waiting to be fed the better. Fast food is tailor-made for a fast life.

But why does life have to be fast? Are you really getting ahead by rushing things all the time? Or is it a case of more haste, less speed?

There is a vast amount of evidence that our time-poor lifestyle is not good for us at all. It creates unending stress, social isolation, careless mistakes, unhappiness, and illness. You can't deliver quality by rushing things. That's a fact that applies to work, play, relationships… and eating.

Eating is not a mundane function that simply needs to be fulfilled three times a day as quickly as possible. It is designed to be a pleasure, a feast for the senses, as well as an opportunity to step off the treadmill, take a pause, socialize, unwind.

For the sake of your mental health, try to take time over meals. Use them as a time to sit down together with friends or family, relax, chat, and enjoy your food. When you take time over food, you not only enjoy the food and the occasion more, you also eat more healthily. You pay more attention to the flavor of the food you eat and you become better connected to your hunger gauge.

Hunger takes time to register. By eating slowly, you give your hunger gauge a chance to tell you when you've had enough. How many times have you kept eating because you haven't felt full and then felt horribly bloated half an hour later?

Give your hunger gauge a chance to respond to the food you're eating and it will tell you when to stop before it's too late.

2. It's convenient

Being time-poor, we often need food that doesn't take ages to prepare, that we can get hold of wherever we are, that we can carry around. But is junk food really that convenient? Don't you have to buy it from a store, just like every other type of food? Or travel to a fast-food restaurant and line up to place your order? Or call for a takeout and wait for it to be delivered?

Is preparing good food really less convenient than all that? Most balanced meals, including fresh, nutritious vegetables, take at least 10 to 15 minutes to prepare. This again is an opportunity to slow down, unwind, and chat. For portability, what could be more convenient than your own packed lunch? You can carry it with you and eat it wherever and whenever you choose. Put in some fruit, salad vegetables, and a few nuts and seeds and you'll find it's tasty and nutritious too.

3. It's cheap

There is a general assumption, even among some healthy-eating advocates, that healthy food costs more than junk food. Scan the supermarket aisles and there are always deals enticing you to stock up on potato chips, chocolate, cookies, and ready meals.

You can get a burger meal for far less than a restaurant serving full, balanced meals.

But are you really comparing like with like? Is the value of food about quantity or quality? The hunger gauge isn't responding to the sheer volume of food you consume; it's looking for the nutritional content. So when you compare the cost of food, you really have to take into account the nutritional content: How much will you need to satisfy your hunger?

With junk food you need a lot more. In fact, a lot of junk food doesn't register on the hunger gauge at all. You must know people who say, "I could eat potato chips all night." That's because those chips never make them feel satisfied—there simply isn't the necessary nutritional content to assuage hunger. Do you find yourself ever eating just one small bag of chips?

Next time you're feeling hungry and want a snack, consider having a piece of fruit instead. Not only is it better for you, but you can also usually save yourself money. Compare the price of a chocolate bar or bag of chips with that of an apple or banana. You'll find the junk food is actually more expensive and it won't leave you feeling satisfied. In fact, most of the time after eating it you probably feel wretched about yourself.

4. It tastes great

This is the real reason why we eat junk, isn't it? We know it's "naughty," we know it's bad for our health, we even know that it doesn't leave us feeling truly satisfied, but oh the taste! That cream cake, that chocolate bar, those fries… Irresistible!

But how much attention do you really pay to the food you eat? Remember the sense test.

How does it look?
How does it smell?
How does it feel?

Does it really excite your senses? Or is there a perception in your brain that is making you salivate? A perception that was put there by a lifetime of brainwashing?

THE ILLUSION OF PLEASURE

What if it were proven that those four arguments for eating junk food were all false? What if the advertising companies announced that these were mere illusions they had conjured up on behalf of the junk food industry? Would that cure your eating problem?

The answer, unfortunately, is no. Because it's not really for these reasons that we get hooked on junk food. The real reason is that we believe that it is giving us some sort of pleasure or comfort. We can't define what that pleasure or comfort is; we just know it's there. And as long as it's there, we find it impossible to unhook from the desire to eat junk.

From childhood, we are brainwashed into thinking that junk food is a treat. We are given candy for being good; there's cake and chocolate on our birthday; we go to fast-food restaurants on special occasions. The message is clear: This food is special. It becomes our favorite food.

Later in life, when we're feeling low, we seek comfort from our favorites. As a child you may have been rationed in your consumption of candy, cookies, and cakes, but when you're an adult with your own money and your own rules, the rationing ends. You can indulge yourself whenever you feel like it. And the more you indulge yourself, the more you feel like it.

BECAUSE IT'S ADDICTIVE!

It's like an itch that you can't resist scratching. If you don't scratch it, then the itch nags away at you; if you do, the itch gets worse. As long as you believe that the only way to stop the itch is to scratch it, you will keep scratching it and the itch will keep getting worse.

This is the cycle of addiction. As the itch gets worse, your scratching becomes less effective. So you have to scratch harder. The scratching isn't making you happy and relaxed, but you're convinced that if you don't scratch, the itch will be unbearable.

Addiction traps you in a cycle of trying to get relief by using the very thing that's causing you misery. It plays tricks on your mind and creates its own need. The only way to stop the cycle of misery is to stop scratching the itch.

HOW CAN I STOP EATING?

Smokers and vapers who quit with Easyway learn that the only way to quit is to cut out cigarettes and nicotine completely. There is no scope for having "just the one" every so often because "just the one" is enough to get you hooked all over again. Not having another cigarette or e-cigarette is easy to do because smoking or vaping, or any form of nicotine addiction, does nothing for you whatsoever. Therefore, the illusion of pleasure is easy to dispel. It only takes around five hours at our live seminars.

But when it comes to emotional eating, this point needs to be explained more carefully. I began the chapter by saying that eating should be a pleasure. So how do you tell real pleasure from illusory pleasure? Later I will give you a practical demonstration that will show you how; for now, I can assure you that you obviously won't be required to stop eating; you won't even be expected to cut down. All you need to do is change your perception of the foods you eat.

To do that, you need to follow the second instruction.

SECOND INSTRUCTION:
OPEN YOUR MIND

You may already regard yourself as an open-minded person. The fact is we go through life with our minds largely made up by other people. When you see the sun rise in the morning, you regard it as a ball of fiery gases burning millions of miles away that has the appearance of rising in the sky because the Earth is turning. But how do you know that's the case? Isn't it because you've been presented with some very convincing arguments by people who you regard as experts in that field, and the explanation tallies with what you see with your own eyes?

But not very long ago, people were convinced that the sun was actually a god driving a fiery chariot across the sky. That was the explanation put forward by the learned men of the time and it tallied with what people saw.

Now take a look at the three men below.

If I were to tell you that the men shown in this diagram are all exactly the same size, you'd dispute that, wouldn't you? The fact is they *are* all identical. Take a ruler and measure them if you need to be convinced.

This illusion demonstrates how our minds can easily be tricked into accepting false "facts." When you first started "comfort eating," you probably believed you were exercising your freedom to choose what you wanted to eat and when, but what if you were basing your choice on false information?

As you continue through the book, remember these men—and keep an open mind, so that even if I tell you something that you find difficult to believe, you will accept the possibility that it could be true.

Chapter 3

WHY YOU'RE READING THIS BOOK

Whenever you're not eating, you always have food on your mind, but whenever you are eating, do you wish you weren't? This is the paradox of emotional eating. Why is it so hard to stop even when you derive no pleasure from it?

IN HER OWN WORDS: SARAH, NEW YORK

My issues with binge-eating and food restricting really developed in my mid-teens and early 20s. Prior to that I was a pretty normal kid. I ate junk food but wasn't obsessed with it or my weight. I wasn't very much into my looks: I was slim, often wore baggy clothes, and the thought of wearing a dress was my worst nightmare.

I was doing well in junior high school and had a great circle of friends. I had a relatively stress-free life during that time and felt pretty happy. A long stay with my mother (who came in and out of my life quite randomly) the summer before I went to college changed all of that.

I had always enjoyed her cooking—it was incredibly carb- and meat-centric. She'd make it during the day whenever I stayed with her. When she didn't feel like cooking, she'd take me out to the local Chinese restaurant, Indian restaurant, or Jamaican takeout (as a kid she'd take me to a pizza place where I could eat an unlimited amount because I was under ten years old). Our time together always centered around food.

That summer I had stayed with her for six weeks straight, a much longer time than usual, and she started feeding me up. Being a teen with a big appetite, I didn't complain, and she enjoyed making sure I was well fed.

Eating that way with little exercise, however, took a toll on my body and I returned to my dad's house almost 25 pounds heavier. I felt incredibly uncomfortable in my skin. The first thing a friend of mine mentioned was "Your belly's sticking out." I hadn't seen the friend since before the summer break, so it was more noticeable to them. I blushed; it was the first time I really cared about what someone else thought of my appearance.

Once I started college, I struggled to shed the weight, but I carried on and was doing OK until my second year of studying. Academically, I was OK, but I struggled with my mom being around again (we had years of unresolved issues to deal with) and my dad was moving abroad to start a new job. He had always been there for me, the one constant in my life. I felt upended when he left, and things became worse when I moved in with my mother. I was going through the emotional mill and, never one to express any negative feelings (for fear of upsetting others), I didn't confide in my friends or family. I kept it all bottled up for years.

As a result, my binge-eating got worse. I was eating to make myself feel better, not realizing that I was only making things worse. I used to go to the local Chinese takeout near college for lunch, then on to the fried chicken joint on my way home at the end of the day. On bad days, I bought a family-sized bucket of fried chicken, and was too embarrassed to eat it in public. Once I got home, I'd hurriedly set up my food on the living room floor, switch on the television, and dive into it, mindlessly gorging, until I hit the bottom of the bucket.

Essentially, I was zoning out, switching off, and always felt disappointed when there was no food left. It seemed like it was the only time I'd have an hour to myself, where I'd stop worrying or having to think about my uncertain future.

At this time, my problem with binge-eating was at an all-time high and I was fed up with feeling lethargic, heavy, bloated, and sick. I felt a slave to what I was eating, and the taste was no longer enjoyable. I needed to lose weight, and lots of it, in an incredibly short amount of time. My solution was to stop eating.

I went down to one tiny meal a day and the results seemed great at first. I enjoyed feeling my clothes grow baggy on me. I was also getting compliments from my friends and, when my dad came back for a visit, he was happy to see I looked "well." No one knew about the starvation tactics I was using. Inside, I felt terrible.

I could only go for so long starving myself and once I'd lost a significant amount of weight, I went straight back to binge-eating, forgetting that that had been my original problem.

I'd kept my "diet" secret from my mom, and she seemed happy that I was back to eating "properly" again. Meanwhile, I ballooned quickly to several sizes bigger than before. I felt shame, embarrassment, and hugely disappointed with myself. What would my friends say when I saw them again? (At this point in my life, I often avoided going out and would go for weeks without seeing anyone.) What would my dad think?

So I yo-yoed back to the starvation tactics, only this time it seemed harder. After a long day at college, I stopped by the local grocery store and bought chocolate-dipped cornflakes and brownie bites from the bakery department. They both came in large plastic containers. I had every intention of just taking a mouthful from each box. I put them on the kitchen counter, prised open the lids, and had a taste of each. I stood there trying to enjoy the sickly-sweet flavor with each small bite, but they were gone pretty quickly. My eyes lingered on the boxes packed with "treats." I convinced myself that taking another little bit wouldn't do any harm. Of course, one thing led to another, and another, until finally I gave in and ate both boxes in one go. I was almost out of breath by the time each box was empty.

I felt sick to my stomach and ashamed. I had spent weeks using every ounce of willpower not to eat, only to throw it all away again and stuff my face with 2,000 calories of junk. Sad to say, I had become such an expert in counting calories that I knew exactly how much I had consumed in less than ten minutes.

What happened next felt so normal that I barely gave it a thought. I was alone in the house and headed straight for the toilet. I purged all of my intake, along with whatever else I had eaten earlier that day. Instantly, I equated the feeling of emptiness, the feeling of being lighter, and the rush to my head, as "feeling better." I felt I had "regained control" and I did not feel guilty about what I had done. In some distorted way, I felt it was natural getting rid of the junk I had consumed like this. I began to think of it as my "get out of jail free card."

If I had moments of indulgence, I could purge myself immediately. It became addictive, chasing after that empty feeling, and regaining what I thought was control. This only came about after I had consumed processed foods (oddly enough I didn't ever feel the urge to purge healthy foods). I know the idea of purging crosses people's minds from time to time; all I can say is it nearly destroyed me and it achieves the exact opposite of what you hope. It doesn't put you in control; it takes control away from you.

I'd been running around in circles like that for years when my dad moved back to New York I decided to move back in with him once I finished college. Life had felt stressful and tough without him and I craved stability. I hadn't had that for almost four years (which I had mostly spent binge-eating, purging, and calorie restricting).

At home with my dad and sisters, we took turns cooking. Doing this forced me to think of others and put their needs before my own, and so I became more interested in the foods I chose to cook. They were always healthy, wholesome meals full of vegetables and salad.

The purging episodes became fewer and farther apart as I started consuming fewer processed foods. I became calmer again.

I realized eating that way I didn't have to feel guilty and some days I wouldn't count the calories I was consuming and most days I didn't even think about purging (let alone doing it). I had also stopped starving myself.

When I think about it, I had developed an unhealthy relationship with junk food based around an incredibly stressful and emotional time in my life and it would take me years to dig myself out of it. I realized the binge-eating and food restricting did not help me deal with my emotions and anxiety, but only triggered them and made me feel worse. It did not change the fact I felt anxious or upset, and lonely. It was no consolation at all.

When I read Allen Carr's *Good Sugar Bad Sugar*, a lot of elements slotted into place for me. I learned I could enjoy what I eat by creating a healthy relationship with food and seeing Bad Sugar for what it is: Poison.

As a result, most of the anxiety I had been suffering for years disappeared. But it only happened once I had stopped consuming Bad Sugar and could finally feel good in myself. Essentially, the book provided me with all the answers, and helped me create a positive attitude toward food that I had never enjoyed before.

BRAINWASHING

Emotional eating takes all the pleasure out of eating. Every time you indulge your craving it makes you miserable and you desperately wish you could quit. The excitement that we're born to feel when anticipating a genuinely tasty treat disappears as a result of eating junk and eating just becomes a conflicted or even mundane experience, leaving you with a low, sinking feeling. So why don't emotional eaters who have become bored with the food they eat just stop? The reason lies in the way our brains are wired. While your rational mind may tell you that the way you eat is causing you harm and misery and that you must stop, your emotional mind continues to crave junk food. Why? Because it has been conditioned to believe that junk food is the only thing that can give you pleasure or comfort. This creates a tug-of-war between two fears: the fear of what emotional eating is doing to you versus the fear of life without what you perceive to be your little crutch. It's a revelation to some people when they realise that both ends of this tug-of-war are caused by the same thing: Emotional eating.

There's only one way to break free and allow your rational mind to regain control: The easy way. You have to undo the brainwashing that creates the desire for junk food and break free from the addiction keeping you enslaved. Before you can begin this process, however, you need to insure you're in the right frame of mind. That means two things:

1. Recognize and accept that you have been brainwashed.

2. Take a positive attitude to escaping from the trap.

The difference between Easyway and all the other methods that claim to help overcome addiction is that the other methods begin with the message that it will not be easy. This has the effect of acting as another piece of brainwashing that unwittingly keeps addicts in the trap, because the harder you think quitting is going to be, the more fearful you will be of trying, and the more you will seek comfort in the "devil you know."

THE BELIEF THAT QUITTING WILL BE HARD KEEPS EMOTIONAL EATERS IN THE TRAP, DESPITE KNOWING THAT IT IS DOING THEM HARM

The obvious question is this:

IF IT'S EASY TO STOP, WHY DOESN'T EVERYONE DO IT?

It's important to ask questions like this and not just to swallow everything you're told. I want you to question everything you're told about the food you eat and that includes everything you've ever been told in the past. When you question things, the truth will be revealed. The problem is that most of us never question the information that is put around about food from generation to generation.

Easyway works. Millions of ex-addicts around the world can vouch for that. At this stage, it doesn't matter if you're ready to believe it or not; all that matters is that you follow the instructions. After all, what have you got to lose? The further loss of control, deterioration of your health, and more misery? Let's examine the reasons why you believe that quitting will be hard.

THE "PROOF" OF FAILURE

You probably know of other people who have tried to get their eating problem under control but failed. Perhaps you have tried yourself, but found yourself pulled back into the trap by a force that was too strong for you to overcome.

Every failed attempt to quit an addiction is damaging for two reasons. The first is the effect it has on your self-esteem. Already low because of the helplessness you feel as an addict, every failure gives your self-esteem a further battering. You see it as an indictment of yourself and a sign of your own weak character.

Secondly, failure reinforces your belief that your addiction is an impregnable prison from which it is incredibly hard to escape.

This second impression can be caused not just by your own failure to quit but also the failure of others. Every time you hear of someone who has made an attempt to stop but failed, it reinforces your belief that stopping is incredibly hard.

When you look at these people, and even when you look at yourself, you see someone who is, in many ways, strong. There is no "type" that becomes an addict because they are weak or foolish or too stupid to see their way out of their problem. Many highly intelligent, single-minded, brave, and strong people have suffered the misery of addiction and found it impossible to escape. The reason they find it so hard to escape is not because it is hard, but because they are going about it the wrong way.

LOSING THE WILL

You cannot escape the trap without a positive attitude. You might interpret that as "I need to muster all my willpower." Many people make this assumption, but it is a false one and it actually drives addicts further into the trap. We shall go into this in greater detail later, but for now just take on board the idea that you do not need willpower to overcome your eating problem.

People who try to stop and fail usually assume that they have failed because they lack the willpower to resist the temptation to eat their favorite foods—even when those foods no longer give them any pleasure.

They believe that it must be some weakness on their part that prevents them from quitting permanently.

This is another misconception that is put in your mind by brainwashing—and not only by the people who want you to remain addicted. Most methods that claim to help control addiction begin from the position that willpower is essential. Easyway has always been the one method that does not. It also happens to be the most effective method ever devised.

I said that this book will help you to overcome your eating problem without any sense of sacrifice or deprivation. When you reach the end and experience the elation of finding yourself free, you will know exactly what I mean. Right now, however, you may still be finding it hard to believe that it is possible to overcome your eating problem without huge amounts of willpower and a painful period of withdrawal.

You have a simple choice:

1. Keep reading and following the instructions and see if my claim is valid;

2. Or continue the way you're going now, suffering the misery of emotional eating, falling deeper and deeper into the trap, losing your health, your body shape, your self-respect, and becoming increasingly resigned to a miserable fate.

If you think you've failed to quit in the past because you lack the willpower, I have nothing but good news for you. You didn't need willpower. You failed to quit because you were using a method that does not work. By picking up this book, you have embarked on a method that has been proven to work by millions of people around the world. Whether it's nicotine addiction, cocaine, heroin, cannabis, prescription drugs, alcohol, or sugar addiction (these are all perceived as mainly physically addictive issues), or gambling, junk-spending, digital/tech addiction, or emotional eating (for the most part perceived as mainly mentally addictive issues), this method has set tens of millions of people free. Easily! All you have to do is keep reading and following all the instructions. It really is as easy as that!

WHAT AM I WITHOUT MY FOOD?

It sounds like a peculiar question, but for some overeaters a reputation for gluttony feel like a key part of identity. Whereas some, if not most, overeaters conduct a lot of their overeating in secret, others parade their excess consumption as a badge of honor, apparently happy to be thought of as accomplished gluttons. References to food intake get an easy laugh and it can lead to individuals almost defining themselves by food—based on what, when, and how much they eat.

This just shows how addiction can twist your mind. You overlook the misery, the ill health, the torment, the self-loathing, and continue to see your problem as some sort of private, or public, charisma.

Of course, you know that's not the real state of affairs. Emotional eaters are anything but happy-go-lucky. They constantly worry about their eating problem, about the physical and mental effects, about the health implications. About being controlled.

Of course, you spend most of your time trying to conceal the fact that you have an eating problem. You put on a brave, smiling face to cover up the misery and confusion. But underneath you are ashamed of the way eating affects you. You don't want everybody to know that you've lost control, that you've lost the ability to enjoy life, and that you're stuck in a trap from which you feel incapable of escape.

You know the truth: There is nothing charming or fun about being addicted to junk food. The effects on your physical health are depressing at best, devastating at worst. The effect on your mental health is to plunge you into a spiral of misery and confusion.

IN HIS OWN WORDS: PAUL

There's a common assumption that people overeat because they weren't brought up with the right guidelines around food; perhaps they were allowed too much candy or overfed at meal times. That certainly wasn't the case with me. My mom cooked great meals and I was fit, slim, and very active until I left home.

It was when I had the freedom of buying my own food that my problems began. I knew that other kids had been allowed things like fast food and chocolate and cakes and I regarded these things as forbidden fruit. Then suddenly I found that I could have them—and have them whenever I wanted. So I indulged myself.

I went on a junk food binge that lasted about three years. I put on 98 pounds and lost interest in all physical pastimes. People have asked me why I didn't stop when I started putting on weight. A good question. Why don't we just stop when we see the damage we're doing? I couldn't understand it either. All I knew was that food was the one thing I wanted when I felt sad about my physical appearance, and every time I tried to stop I failed. Thanks to Easyway, I now understand why I didn't stop. I didn't see the food as the problem; I thought I was the problem. I sought comfort in the food, not realizing that it was the food, not me, that was the cause of my misery.

Easyway gave me the power to see that and to stop blaming myself. As soon as I changed my mindset, I was able to stop eating junk without feeling I was depriving myself and I stopped worrying about a lack of willpower. I'm back to fighting fitness now and, more importantly, I genuinely look forward to mealtimes and enjoy the taste of the food I'm eating—just like I did when my mom did the cooking.

DENIAL

Everyone with an eating problem wishes they could stop. The fact that they find themselves incapable of doing so makes them feel foolish and weak, so they try to make themselves feel better by concocting excuses for why they continue to overeat.

> **"It's just the way I'm made."**
> **"I've got to keep this body fueled."**
> **"I do it to make people laugh."**

These are all examples of how addicts delude themselves. They all imply that you have made a controlled choice to eat in each case. But as everyone with an eating problem knows,

YOU DON'T CONTROL EMOTIONAL EATING; IT CONTROLS YOU

Depending on what kind of emotional eater you are, there may be times when you feel you are exercising control by not caving in to the impulse to binge on food. This sense of control can be intoxicating, in a sense addictive, but when willpower fails it becomes confused and dysfunctional and results in ever-more frequent binges, and ever-increasing periods of overeating. It becomes a vicious cycle that, bound up together in one neat package, is broadly defined as emotional eating. As mentioned, sometimes it can even be the exercise of control for periods of time that is the addictive element and, in other cases, in complete contrast, it can be the abandoning of control (the surrender to a binge) that serves to hook you. In many cases, it is a confusing combination of the two. (These issues are entirely aside from the physical addiction to refined sugar and processed or starchy carbs.)

The three elements of emotional eating addiction are:

   1. *Exercise of control NOT to binge*

   2. *Abandonment of control, succumbing to the impulse to binge*

   3. *Addiction to refined sugar, processed and starchy carbs*

I'm sure that the first element might confuse some. Of course, there's nothing wrong with using discipline and willpower to avoid bingeing on food, other than the fact that it can be exhausting, in virtually all cases impossible to maintain, and therefore destined periodically to fail. More importantly, there's no need to do it.

Once you understand how you've become addicted to emotional eating—the exercise of control is entirely redundant—you'll need no more discipline or willpower or control "not to binge" on a family tub of ice cream than you would need "not to binge" on a plate of raw potato.

Some people who battle issues with food resort to purging (self-induced vomiting, misuse of laxatives, diuretics, or enemas). If you fall into that category, or into the category that continually exercises extreme control in order to avoid a "normal" level of food intake, please follow my advice and reach out to your doctor or one of the amazing charities and organizations that exist to provide non-judgmental kindness, support, guidance, and advice to to people who live with "Other Specified Feeding or Eating Disorder" (OSFED), "Binge Eating Disorder," "Bulimia," or "Anorexia."

No harm can come from doing so and undoubtedly you'll benefit tremendously. Please don't feel let down that in this book we might overlook your specific plight. To address every aspect of emotional eating and also cover issues such as bulimia or anorexia and everything in between would be foolhardy. If you live with these serious issues, my hope is that within the pages of this book you might discover a new understanding and appreciation of your relationship with food and emotions, and that you'll be inspired to reach out to those mentioned above for kindness, guidance, and support.

Fortunately, most people reading this book don't have to live with this, although make no mistake, emotional eating is always extremely unpleasant and debilitating. You feel trapped in a never-ending see-saw battle to control your eating, to limit your bingeing, and the misery of dealing with deeply upsetting feelings of isolation, shame, regret, and remorse that accompany or follow binges.

That's quite aside from the physical symptoms of experiencing frequent cravings for certain foods, or weight gain, of feeling bloated after mealtimes and binges, and experiencing the mood swings, anxiety, and depression that accompany all of these.

Even if you maintain periods of seemingly blissful abandon, not feeling the need or desire to attempt to control your eating—at the back of your mind, there's the nagging thought that you're "out of control" and that sooner or later you need to address the situation.

It's often when you feel at your absolute lowest, when the weight of the world seems to have dragged you to your knees, that the truth confronts you: Virtually all the problems you have, which seem so insurmountable now, so unbearable, so inescapable, whether they are to do with relationships, family, friends, work, or all of the above, are exacerbated and amplified many times over by the fact that your eating (and sometimes your drinking too) are completely out of control.

Losing control over food is guaranteed to make you feel awful. The allure of the stuff is one thing, but how it actually makes you feel once you've consumed it is another thing entirely. There's a good reason it's called junk food.

It's not just food that we normally consider to be junk that causes the problem, stuff from fast-food outlets. There's a whole range of foods that you might be surprised to see on a list of junk food: bread, pasta, potatoes (whether fried, boiled, or baked); in fact all starchy carbs and processed foods make you feel lousy, mentally and physically. Did you ever polish off a bowl of pasta and feel light, energetic, and alive? Or more likely, do you tend to overeat it and feel bloated and lethargic?

Whether it's refined sugar products, chocolate, cakes, pastries, and puddings, or bread products—potato, starchy carbs, rice—there's two simple reasons that you tend to overeat them:

1. They have virtually zero nutritional value, so the brain continues to prompt you to eat more and more in an attempt to reach the required nutritional value to satisfy your hunger.

2. They're addictive!

Collectively, I call those refined sugar and starchy carb foods "Bad Sugar," with the sugar and carbs found in fresh fruit and fresh vegetables being their polar opposite, "Good Sugar."

Thankfully, addiction to Bad Sugar is easy to break. It might be stating the obvious, but once you stop eating them, their attraction completely disappears. That's as long as you understand how the addiction works and as long as you see through the illusion of pleasure that the addiction generates.

So, after a period of "letting yourself go" (which might mean a day, a few days, several weeks, or a month, perhaps even the entire summer vacation or the short breaks at Easter, Christmas, New Year, or any other time when your mental and physical state is at its lowest ebb), you try to exert control again.

You either don't get off first base at all, having "good mornings" but "bad afternoons and evenings", or "good days" and "bad days." There again, perhaps you succeed for a while, then fall off the healthy-eating wagon, then succeed for a bit more, then fall off the wagon again.

And it becomes an on-off-on-off battle. When you feel you're doing well, you kid yourself that all is well and try to ignore the occasional "blip," dismissing it on the basis of "It's been a tough week—I deserve to let my hair down," or "It's my best friend's birthday—I don't want to be a party pooper eating salad," or whatever justification comes into your mind. Or perhaps it might be more honestly described as whatever phoney reason your mind can come up with.

It's a miserable feeling, but if you recognize some, or even all, of the situations I've described, I have only good news for you. Freedom awaits. All you need to do is carry on reading and follow the instructions.

When you're in a trap, it's frightening to admit it. You're faced with two options: Stay in the trap and continue to suffer, or get out. Getting out can seem scarier than staying in if you've been brainwashed into believing it will be a difficult, painful process. Faced with that prospect, the familiarity of the trap seems the lesser of two evils.

But when you realize that getting out need be neither painful nor difficult, the situation changes completely. Rather than facing two evils in a tug-of-war, you find yourself facing one evil and one simple, happy option. That's when escape becomes easy.

THE EASY OPTION

You have a pretty good idea of what life will be like if you choose to remain in the trap. More of the physical degradation, more of the mental torment. Now let's examine the life that awaits you as a "Free Eater."

Health

Overeating affects your health both mentally and physically. Being overweight puts strain on all your vital organs, including your heart and lungs, making the simplest of physical tasks hard work. It creates an addiction cycle in your mind, making it impossible to enjoy genuine pleasures because your brain is always craving the "reward" of a junk food fix. The combination of physical and mental discomfort can cause sleep deprivation. And the worse you feel, the more you neglect all aspects of your health. When you're free from the tyranny of emotional eating, you will start to genuinely enjoy the taste of food again, you will feel fitter and more energetic, you will sleep more soundly, and generally feel a fantastic glow of health and happiness. It's not just physical health which is infinitely improved; it's mental health too. Release from the awful dark cloud of constant bingeing and all the attempts to control what you're eating, with the feelings of repeated failure, of fear, shame, and damaged self-esteem, is like escaping from a cold, dark prison cell —into sunshine, blue sky and freedom.

Control

With something as fundamental as eating back under your control, you will feel so much better about yourself. You will recognize your ability to make the decisions that govern your life and happiness and you will be able to lead a more relaxed lifestyle, free from the constant struggle with food. When I say "back under control," what I should say is "no longer out of control." It's not so much a case of you taking control of what you eat—as much as letting your brain and body do the job they're naturally equipped to do.

Does a squirrel exercise willpower or control over what it eats? Not really. It can naturally tell the difference between food and poison. The same goes for every wild animal in its natural habitat on this planet. They don't eat junk, they don't eat more than they need to, and they go about their business without any nutrition advisors, diet plans, or digital scales.

Honesty

When your eating issue is resolved, you will no longer feel ashamed and compelled to cover up your addiction. As a result, you will feel far less stressed, less defensive, and free from self-doubt with all the harm that does to your self-esteem.

Self-respect

Your new, stress-free lifestyle and the realization that you are no longer a slave to junk will make you feel much better about yourself. Every time you think about your achievement in escaping the trap, you will feel a burst of elation and pride.

Time

You might need to plan your meals with a little more thought and care, but once you're free, it's a liberating process rather than a burden or chore. Being more mindful of what you eat and how you eat it is magical and you'll find that you have more time and the inclination to pursue things you truly enjoy, like taking exercise or just relaxing with family and friends.

Money

Overeating is expensive. So is junk food. You can look forward to much smaller grocery bills when you're not blowing your money on junk that gives you no satisfaction whatsoever.

You have all these benefits, and many more, to look forward to when you walk out of the trap that is emotional eating. In order to get there, you don't need willpower, nor to fight your way through a painful period of withdrawal. All you need to do is keep a positive mindset and methodically unravel the illusions that have put you in the trap in the first place.

It's simply a case of following the instructions, so if you're worried that you're about to be made to go through some awful trauma, or to sacrifice something that is truly precious to you, put that thought out of your mind and replace it with the thought of all the terrific benefits you will soon get to enjoy.

THIRD INSTRUCTION:
BEGIN WITH A FEELING OF ELATION

Chapter 4

FIRST STEPS TO FREEDOM

IN THIS CHAPTER
• *HOW EASYWAY WORKS* • *EATING FOR HEALTH AND PLEASURE*
• *GETTING FREE AND STAYING FREE* • *PRODUCT PROFILE*

The beliefs that keep you trapped in the misery of emotional eating are illusions. There's nothing to fear without your food fixes. Escaping the trap is easy and you have nothing to mope about. This is the truth: Now all we need to do is have you accept it.

When you're desperate to find a cure for a problem like emotional eating, you can start to believe that the only thing that will help you is a miracle. You may have heard that Easyway works like magic and I'm sure you're eager to discover the secret of this magical cure. You're probably wondering why I don't just tell you the magic formula right here and now. Please don't be misled:

1. It's not a secret.

2. There is no magic, even if it seems like there is.

Easyway works by using undisputable logic to strip away the illusions put in your mind by brainwashing and replacing those illusions with rational thought, which removes your desire to use food for emotional relief. The key is the set of instructions you receive throughout the book and it must be used like the combination lock of a safe. Each step must be understood and applied in order for the combination to work.

You already have the first three instructions and your escape plan is well under way, but please be patient. The key to your escape does not lie in the final chapter or the first chapter, or any chapter alone; the whole book is the key.

HOW EASYWAY WORKS

It works by removing your desire to eat junk, or for that matter to eat anything in response to emotions rather than natural appetite and hunger. In order to do that, we need to change your approach to food and emotions. What is it that makes you an emotional eater? It's a subtle combination of addiction to Bad Sugar, the exercise of control NOT to binge, and the abandonment of control, meaning you succumb to the impulse to binge.

It might appear slightly perverse to list the exercise of control "not to binge" as being part of the problem. After all, most people would consider it simply a matter of lack of control that causes emotional eating. Yet without periods of control, there cannot be moments of loss of control.

If you consider a "normal" eating pattern, it is, within certain parameters, a fairly flat, steady line. By and large, that's how the animal kingdom eats, including those humans you might consider to be "normal eaters."

An emotional eater endures an eating pattern which is full of highs and lows, peaks and troughs… periods of *restraint* during which they might feel deprived and miserable, interrupted by periods of *loss of restraint*.

These periods of *loss of restraint* drag us down even lower, and make us feel even more wretched. It is the ending of a binge, the return to *restrained* normal, controlled eating that seems to provide some sort of comfort or peak. It feels like a peak, yet all it is is a simple return to normality. In fact it's far from normal; it's a virtually constant state of feeling deprived—a feeling that we're missing out on the food we really want and feeling awful about the moments of apparent weakness and gluttony when we binge. There really aren't many happy moments for emotional eaters.

Mixed into this process is the effect of sugar addiction, which causes massive disruptions to our blood sugar levels and makes us feel lousy as we bounce back and forward between unnaturally high blood sugar levels (as a result of consuming Bad Sugar) and unnaturally deep sugar level crashes (again the result of having consumed Bad Sugar).

This cocktail of apparently contradictory sensations and feelings is common in addiction. Cocaine addicts often take cocaine (a stimulant) with alcohol (a depressant) in a deliberate attempt to counteract the other. "I take coke to help me drink more booze and then I drink more booze to get down off the coke" is something we often hear at our cocaine addiction seminars.

It's amazing how many people think that the solution to unnaturally low blood sugar levels (that always follow the unnaturally high blood sugar levels caused by consuming Bad Sugar) is to eat more Bad Sugar… which in turn creates an unnaturally high blood sugar level, which inevitably leads to the discomfort of the next crash.

The result of this distorted eating pattern for many is Type 2 diabetes and the rampant Type 2 diabetes epidemic sweeping across the globe. It's a 21st-century disaster born out of the massive increase in consumption of refined sugar, processed foods, and starchy carbs since the 1980s.

All in all, the emotional eater is in an almost constant state of discomfort.

Either they feel mentally deprived because they can't have what they think they'd *really* like to eat, or suffering from the *basic* physical effects of eating what they thought they'd really like to eat (bloating and weight gain), they endure the *second level* physical effects of sugar addiction (blood sugar level distortion and mood swings) while constantly battling the negative mental effects of the misery and guilt associated with all of the above.

Luckily, with Easyway, you'll soon be able to escape from the whole nightmare of emotional eating.

The key to your escape is to understand that exercising control over what you eat through sheer willpower isn't desirable; instead we should *allow ourselves* to eat healthy food because it's genuinely preferable to junk.

Can you see how the former requires willpower, effort, and control, whereas the latter does not?

EATING FOR HEALTH AND PLEASURE

Don't misunderstand me. I'm not saying that you should try to *kid* yourself into believing that healthy food is infinitely preferable to junk.

I'm saying that once you've understood how Bad Sugar addiction and emotional-eating addiction have fooled you into eating food that is bad for you, you'll no longer feel in any way deprived if you don't eat the kinds of foods which, deep down, you already know do you harm.

This book will help release you from the emotional eating trap. Food is never a good response to a psychological problem—to stress, to loneliness, to sadness, or to heartbreak. The only thing food is a useful response to is…

GENUINE HUNGER

This method will remove those impulses from your way of thinking and let logic and reason undo the brainwashing to which you've been subjected ever since you were a child.

> ### FALLING BACK IN
> An addict is caught in a trap, like a cage sunk into the ground. Between us we have the two essentials that will set you free: You have a strong desire to get out and I have the key that will make that possible. All you have to do is follow the instructions.
>
> However, once you are released, there is a further danger: The trap still exists and we have to insure that you do not fall into it again.

GETTING FREE AND STAYING FREE

People with addictions like emotional eating are notorious for stopping and starting again. They make a big effort to quit or cut down and then, when they feel they've regained some degree of control, they reward themselves with a little binge. "Just the one, what's the harm?" The harm is that "just the one" is all it takes to push you back into the trap.

So getting you out of the trap is not enough; we need to insure you never fall into it again.

We can do this by making sure you understand the nature of the trap. This is not something that society generally talks about. We don't like to think that we might be caught in a trap. We like to think we're in control. So we allow the brainwashing to go unchallenged and it warps our perception of how things really are. But until you recognize the trap and question the brainwashing, you cannot truly escape the slavery of being an emotional eater.

Unlike the cage in the ground, the trap you're in is not a physical trap but a psychological one. In other words, it exists entirely in your mind. It is an illusion conjured up by brainwashing.

THE TRAP IS VERY EASY TO FALL INTO...
AND JUST AS EASY TO ESCAPE

Remember the picture illusion in Chapter 2? All it takes is one false piece of information to make you believe that what you're looking at is three men of exactly the same size. When it comes to the food you eat, you have been brainwashed with similar false impressions that have created the illusion that you get some sort of pleasure or comfort from it. Therefore, you believe that going without it will mean deprivation and misery.

It's a confidence trick—and once you see through a confidence trick you never fall for it again. Try turning back to that picture with the knowledge you now have. Can you convince yourself that the men are not identical?

Why does the brainwashing trap some people and not others? Millions of people have lived their lives without ever falling into the emotional eating trap, even though they too have been subjected to the brainwashing from a young age.

One theory is that some people are born with an addictive personality. In other words, something in their mentality makes them more vulnerable to falling into the trap. The addictive personality theory is frequently cited as if it were a proven fact, but it is nothing more than a theory and, as I will show you later in the book, there is much ammunition with which to shoot it down. Furthermore, it is of no help whatsoever to addicts trying to escape the trap.

The fact is anybody can fall into the trap and anybody can escape. It's a simple question of understanding what it is that makes you fall in and what it is that keeps you there. No one forces you to eat junk. You choose to do so yourself.

The fact that part of your brain wishes you didn't, or can't understand why you do, doesn't change the situation. You eat junk in response to emotions because you have a desire to do so. Desire is what makes you feel deprived when you force yourself to go without. Desire is what makes you feel agitated when you see other people eating junk food and you seemingly can't. Desire is what drags you back into the trap just when you think you've escaped.

IN ORDER TO STAY OUT OF THE TRAP PERMANENTLY, YOU NEED TO REMOVE THE DESIRE

The only difference between emotional eaters and people who aren't suffering that misery is that the latter don't have the same desire for food as an emotional crutch. That is not to say they are immune to the brainwashing. Somewhere in their minds they too will believe that there is some pleasure or comfort to be gained from eating junk food.

And there may come a time in their lives when they are feeling low and need something to pick them up and they will fall into the same trap as you. It's easy for people to fall into the emotional eating trap, even if they've avoided doing so their entire lives.

For now, though, when they weigh up the pros and cons of emotional eating (if they ever even consider it), they conclude that there is no sense in inflicting that misery on themselves. Without the desire for a food fix, they are able to make that rational decision. They are able to maintain the power of reason over temptation because their reasoning has not been affected by addiction.

Before you despair that you are in no position to apply that sort of reasoning, I have good news for you. You don't need to.

EASYWAY DOES NOT REQUIRE THE POWER OF REASON TO OUTWEIGH TEMPTATION; IT REMOVES TEMPTATION ALTOGETHER

People who have never fallen into the trap are still susceptible to the illusion that there is some pleasure or comfort to be derived from eating junk food and, as importantly, eating junk food in response to emotions. There is no guarantee that at some point in the future they won't succumb to the brainwashing and fall into the trap themselves.

But when you've been in the trap and then removed the brainwashing, you are in a stronger position than someone who has never been trapped: You are no longer susceptible to the illusions.

You KNOW that there is no pleasure or comfort in emotional eating, quite the reverse. Therefore, your desire is removed for good.

The only relevant difference between you and someone who does not use food for emotional support is that they don't have the desire to do so. Neither did you until you fell into the trap.

THE ADDICTION CREATES THE DESIRE

Remember, addicts seek comfort in the very thing that's causing them misery. They just can't see the connection. This is the trap you are in. It is a vicious circle, but you can break it by opening your mind and unraveling the brainwashing.

Thanks to Easyway, there are large numbers of ex-addicts who once thought they could never get free from the trap they were in but have now escaped and have no desire to fall back in.

Soon you will join them.

PRODUCT PROFILE

I've compared emotional eating to drug addiction. Let's explore this comparison further. Here's a description of one of the world's most common addictive substances:

• Well-known for its harmful effects on the human body.

• Usually hooks its victims immediately and in many cases they remain hooked for life.

• Dealers hook users and keep them hooked with cheap deals.

• The more miserable it makes you, the greater your feeling of dependency becomes.

• Side-effects include gum rot, sluggishness, depression, diabetes, stress, anxiety, mood swings, loss of self-esteem, shame, guilt, isolation, and sometimes suicide.

• Benefits: There are none!

This reads like a description of a Class A drug. In fact, as you've probably suspected in spite of me omitting the "weight gain" symptom, it's a description of refined sugar. But it's not the popular image of sugar, is it? We assume it's a description of heroin or some other hard drug because we automatically associate those drugs with their harmful effects and see their addiction for the vile, pitiful, deadly condition that it is.

We don't see sugar in quite the same light, despite knowing very well that it rots our teeth, makes us put on weight and, increasingly, leads to diabetes or serious ill health. The worst we can say about sugary foods is that they're "naughty but nice." Diabetes kills far more people than heroin. Would you call heroin "naughty but nice?"

You need to understand that the trap you're in as an emotional eater is the same as that of a heroin addict.

It's a mental trap, not a physical one, and it is created by brainwashing. In order to escape you need to change your frame of mind. But first it is essential to realize that you are in the trap.

It's easy to recognize the heroin trap. The media portrayal of heroin is quite clear: ADDICTION! SLAVERY! POVERTY! MISERY! DEGRADATION! DEATH!

But the media portrayal of junk food and refined sugar is completely different. Happy, beautiful people, smiling and laughing, showing no signs of tooth decay or obesity or anxiety or depression, just having fun and getting on.

The message is clear: "Junk food makes you happy."

As you read through this book, we will remove these illusions from your brain so that instead of seeing emotional eating as a pleasure or comfort, you start to see the true picture, just as you can with heroin. By the time you finish the book, your frame of mind will be complete, such that whenever you think about using junk food, or any food, for emotional support, instead of feeling deprived because you can *no longer do so*, you will feel overjoyed because you *no longer have to*.

Chapter 5

THE TRAP

Living with emotional eating is like being in a trap, where the more you struggle to break free, the tighter the bonds become. In order to escape, you need to understand how the trap works. When you can see that, escape becomes easy.

You might find it hard to accept that emotional eating is an addiction. We know that junk food isn't healthy, but we don't put it in the same category as heroin, or even nicotine, which everybody knows are addictive drugs and seriously harmful. How can something as commonplace as "food" be addictive?

Bear in mind that 50 years ago, the majority of the adult population regarded smoking in the same way. Even in the early days of Easyway, back in the late 1980s, we faced quite a challenge convincing smokers that they were, in fact, addicted to nicotine. They considered addiction in the same way as they might consider someone being a "golf addict" or "TV addict"—more of a case of liking something a lot rather than being clinically addicted. They were extremely resistant to the notion that they smoked because they were addicted.

These days smokers are more open to that idea; the only challenge that remains for us is having them understand that it's the addiction that convinces them that they enjoy, or gain some kind of benefit from, smoking. Addiction is a confidence trick that has otherwise bright, intelligent, logical people fooled into thinking that they get something positive from a substance that

a) creates unpleasant withdrawal symptoms when it is first taken

b) then partially relieves those unpleasant symptoms when taken for a second time

c) and a third time

d) and a fourth, and so on.

In other words, it's a lifetime chain of slavery.

Addiction to anything involves no more enjoyment than wearing tight shoes for the relief of taking them off. Don't misunderstand me: We've all worn a pair of uncomfortable shoes because we like the way they look, but you simply wouldn't wear shoes that are too tight every day just to experience the relief of taking them off.

Back in the 1960s and 1970s, most people smoked and, even though there was growing evidence that smoking caused cancer, they regarded smoking as much safer than heroin. Yet we know now that smoking is a far bigger killer than heroin.

That's because far more people smoke than take heroin, you might argue. Sure, but why do people do either when they know it's likely to kill them? Is it because of the incredible pleasure or comfort they get from it? Or is it simply because they're addicted to the drug?

WHETHER OR NOT YOU CHOOSE TO SEE YOUR PROBLEM AS ADDICTION, IT DOESN'T ALTER THE FACT OF THE MATTER, WHICH IS THAT JUNK FOOD AND EATING IN RESPONSE TO EMOTIONS RATHER THAN HUNGER TRAPS YOU IN A CYCLE OF CRAVING, DISSATISFACTION, AND SELF-LOATHING IN JUST THE SAME WAY AS ILLICIT DRUGS DO

Back when smoking was at its peak, we didn't know how nicotine and other drugs affected the brain. Since then we have learned a great deal about a function of the brain known colloquially as "reward pathways".

These all depend on dopamine; in the brain dopamine functions as a neurotransmitter, a chemical released by neurons (nerve cells) to send signals to other nerve cells.

The reward pathways play a major role in the motivational component of reward-motivated behavior. Can you imagine the disruption that can be caused to this natural, instinctive process by the introduction of a highly addictive drug that appears to relieve the discomfort its very first dose, and every subsequent dose, creates?

THE TRUTH ABOUT DOPAMINE

It's of tremendous comfort to everyone working within my Easyway organization, who for decades have been working tirelessly to cure addiction all over the world, that as more and more becomes known about the way nicotine influences dopamine, science confirms what Easyway has been saying for more than 35 years. In 2019, one of the world's leading academics in the field of nicotine addiction, Professor Robert West, stated publicly, "Nicotine causes dopamine release by nerve cells in the *nucleus accumbens*, a part of the brain involved in learning to do things. The dopamine release tells the brain to pay attention to the situation and what the smoker was just doing—and to do the same thing next time they're in that same situation. So a link is forged between the impulse to smoke and situations in which smoking normally happens." Professor West went on to add, "Crucially, the smoker doesn't have to feel any pleasure or enjoyment for this to work."

A smoker's first experience of nicotine is normally at worst extremely unpleasant, and at best a little unpleasant. For the sake of understanding this, smokers have to ignore the feelings aroused by the circumstances surrounding their first cigarette: The peer pressure and praise, the feeling of rebelliousness, the desire to fit in, the sense of feeling stylish, sophisticated, or macho. None of these are caused by the introduction of nicotine to the body; they're all to do with the environment and the circumstances in which it was administered.

Most smokers remember the actual physical effect of their first cigarettes as being unpleasant and this alone disproves the notion that nicotine's introduction to the body and brain causes "pleasure." Whatever impact nicotine has on dopamine levels when first introduced to the body, it's certainly not pleasurable.

In fact, most people's first cigarette is so unpleasant and unrewarding it convinces them they could never become addicted. The reason smokers develop a deep-seated belief that smoking IS pleasurable is explained perfectly by Professor

West. It also helps us understand why we become addicted to emotional eating.

I apologise for laboring this point about nicotine and dopamine, and I would forgive you for wondering why on earth I'm boring you with it, but as you'll discover later, it's key to understanding how you've been trapped by emotional eating.

POINT A

Nicotine withdrawal is the result of the first-ever cigarette a nicotine addict smoked. It is momentarily "relieved" by the next cigarette. The brain concludes unconsciously, "Next time you feel nicotine withdrawal—do that again!" In other words, the behavior of lighting a cigarette in response to experiencing nicotine withdrawal is reinforced every time a smoker lights a cigarette regardless of the fact that the next cigarette will also cause nicotine withdrawal.

Whether a smoker is in a happy situation, a concentration situation, a sad situation, a stress situation, a relaxing situation, a boring situation, or a lonely situation, they simultaneously experience nicotine withdrawal, and respond by lighting a cigarette, thereby immediately feeling better than a moment before, and oblivious to the fact that *that* cigarette will perpetuate nicotine withdrawal once it has been smoked.

It's no wonder they think cigarettes help them to be happy or to concentrate, or to cope with sadness and stress, and help them relax or cope with boredom or loneliness! It's got nothing to do with *genuine* pleasure or *genuine* improvement of mood. And every single time they light a cigarette in one of those situations, the brain concludes, "Next time that happens—do that again!"

Nonsmokers don't have to deal with any of the mental and physical aggravation of being addicted to nicotine. They don't suffer nicotine poisoning, nicotine withdrawal, or the unnatural impact nicotine has on dopamine and their behavior.

POINT B

All a smoker is trying to achieve when they light a cigarette is to recapture the feeling of peace, calm, and tranquillity they enjoyed their entire lives before they lit their first experimental cigarette. In other words, a smoker smokes in order to feel like a nonsmoker.

At our live seminars, once a nicotine addict understands Point A and Point B, we explain how nicotine addiction, irrespective of nicotine's influence on dopamine levels, is actually extremely mild, and that the really unpleasant symptoms a smoker suffers when they try to quit without Easyway's help are the result of a mental struggle. That struggle is caused by the smoker feeling deprived of what they think is a genuine pleasure or crutch.

Easyway goes on to reveal how smokers' belief system toward smoking—that it helps them to relax, socialize, handle stress, concentrate, enjoy alcohol, take a break from work, and so on—is based on misinformation and misinterpretation of personal experiences, and their addiction to nicotine.

The smoker then concludes that there aren't any advantages to smoking and therefore there is no point in doing it. This leaves the smoker to handle the extremely mild symptoms of nicotine withdrawal without having to experience the discomfort of feeling that they are missing out on something they used to think they enjoyed or received benefit from.

This is hugely important as the former smoker develops new responses to those old habitual triggers to smoke in the first few weeks of being a happy nonsmoker. For example, if they used to light a cigarette as they left work in the afternoon, that might be a moment when the thought of smoking crosses their mind, but once they quit with Easyway, instead of consciously processing thoughts and feelings of loss, they process thoughts and feelings of release and freedom. They rewire their brain. And it's not only easy—it's enjoyable.

Now, as someone who has suffered with emotional eating, try to apply the thinking above to your own experiences. Think about your relationship with particular foods such as cakes, pastries, candy, cookies, chocolate, ice cream or savories, bread, pizza (bread again!), pasta, and starchy carbs such as potatoes and rice. They're all addictive Bad Sugar foods. When you've experienced sadness, or loneliness, or stress, or any negative emotion, which foods have you found yourself reaching for?

Would it surprise you to know that Bad Sugar impacts on dopamine in a similar way to nicotine? There is a little more complexity to feelings of sugar withdrawal than nicotine withdrawal—for one it has more to do with changes in blood sugar levels—but if you can accept that as a Bad Sugar addict, you reach for Bad Sugar in any tricky situation and in exactly the same way as a smoker and you DO feel better than a moment before, then you're halfway to freedom from emotional eating already.

It's no wonder you think Bad Sugar foods help you to be happy or to concentrate, or to cope with sadness and stress, or to help you relax, or cope with boredom, or loneliness! It has nothing to do with genuine pleasure or genuine improvement of mood. And every single time you've eaten addictive junk at those times—the brain concludes, unconsciously, "Next time you feel that way—DO THAT AGAIN!"

GOOD INTENTIONS

We attempt to remedy the feelings of misery, shame, remorse, guilt, and self-loathing that immediately follow binges by making a concerted, mental undertaking to stop eating junk, to eat healthily, and to reform our eating patterns. It is this process that I referred to earlier when highlighting the involvement of "exercise of control not to binge" in emotional eating.

Remember, the three elements of emotional eating addiction:

1. *Exercise of control NOT to binge*

2. *Abandonment of control, succumbing to the impulse to binge*

3. *Addiction to refined sugar, processed and starchy carbs*

After all this talk of dopamine, you'd be forgiven for thinking that it's a mysterious, elusive, extremely rare, difficult to obtain, magical potion. You couldn't be more wrong.

There are lots of wonderful, enjoyable, thoroughly lovely, safe, non-addictive (entirely free of charge) ways to stimulate dopamine levels in entirely positive ways: Listening to music, dancing, exercise, cuddling up with a friend, a loved one, or a pet, holding hands, laughing, or making love—the list goes on and on. Each of these activities does this. It reads like the recipe for a happy life, doesn't it? There's no secret to it; maybe we should do more of these things, more often!

Rather than engaging in something that makes you feel miserable, guilty, ashamed, bloated, and full of self-loathing, you can fill your life with things that provide real pleasure. That way, a wonderful future lies ahead of you. I'm saying that once you get back in tune with REAL pleasure, GENUINE sensations of enjoyment, DEEP, MINDFUL (or even shallow) sources of contentment, the thought of interrupting that by bingeing or emotional eating and suffering all the horrible consequences becomes unpalatable. Literally.

After a horrible day at work or a falling out with a friend, what do you really think would genuinely make you feel better? A family-sized tub of ice cream or a lovely, long, nurturing cuddle with your partner? In all seriousness, if you'd choose the ice cream, then maybe you'd better rethink how you feel about your partner. Burying your head in a tub of Ben and Jerry's is no solution to anything. But you don't need me to tell you that.

This book won't directly help you fix any relationships you have that need to be mended, but, like every addict on the planet that Easyway has cured, what you will find, once you've escaped from the clutches of emotional eating, is that you'll immediately feel better equipped to sort out other elements in your life that require attention.

That said, there is one relationship that this book will help you fix: The most important one on this planet, your relationship with yourself.

YOU'VE BEEN FAKING IT

Any "high," any boost, any feeling of comfort you've experienced when you have turned to food in response to emotion rather than as a simple response to hunger has been fake. Phoney. It's the result of a fiendish combination of factors: Repeated, prolonged periods of *"suffering"* (exercising control over your food intake) followed by moments or periods of *"release"* (relinquishing control over your food intake), and the partial, momentary *"relief"* of feelings of withdrawal from sugar (Bad Sugar addiction).

Can you see how that's all like wearing tight shoes simply to experience the relief of taking them off?

DOES IT MATTER THAT IT'S FAKE?

Some addicts understand what we say completely, but ask whether it really matters that the high or boost is fake. As long as they feel better as a result of it, isn't that all that counts?

Fake highs are not enjoyable and, once you understand how they work, even the illusion of enjoyment disappears.

A CAUTIONARY TALE

Imagine you make a new friend. They tell you they've had a bit of luck at work and want to share their success with you. How about a few cocktails after work in a swanky bar? They insist that it's their treat. Given their absolute insistence, you go along with the idea, especially as you're only just managing to make ends meet at the moment. So you have a fabulous "after work" drink with them: The bar is cool and chic, the drinks are beautifully mixed, the music is amazing, and it doesn't cost you a single penny. You go home walking on air having had a great time. At the back of your mind, though, you know your new friend must have spent $75 on drinks, but you resolve to repay the treat next time.

A week passes and the same friend messages you, inviting you out after work. It's exactly the same story as last time; they say they've had an amazing stroke of luck at work and they really want to invite you out to the same bar as last week. They insist on picking up the tab again. They refuse any offers to pay again and insist that you help them celebrate their good fortune. It's another wonderful hour or two, a release from the drudgery of just heading home and sticking to your strict budget. You return home again on a complete high. You can't get over your friend's generosity, but they seemed so happy, so excited, and carefree that this time you didn't even feel guilty afterward. If $75 is nothing to them, then who are you to argue?

The following week, the same thing happens: the invite, the carefree hour or two after work, drinks with a fun friend, and it's a wonderful release from your tight budget, especially as you seem shorter of cash than ever. The same thing happens every week for the next month or two and you feel a deeper and deeper sense of gratitude and appreciation for your friend's constant generosity and kindness. Where would you be without her, especially with money being so tight?

But your money worries worsen and you finally get around to checking your bank statement to work out where you can cut back further to insure you keep your head above water.

To your horror you notice, corresponding with every single one of your after-work drinks, your statement shows a cash withdrawal on your account of $150! You feel sick, a deep sense of shock, and gradually panic turns to anger as you realize that you've been conned.

Somehow, your new "so-called" friend got access to your bank account. It wasn't *her* buying the drinks on those nights out, it was you! She was taking $150 cash out of your account, spending half of it on drinks for you both, and pocketing the rest. She's definitely not a friend;

in fact she's a thief. If there can possibly be something worse than that, she's it. She's a fake, phoney, callous, heartless thief who tricked you into thinking that you were her friend.

Think about it. How would you feel about those after-work drinks now? Would you describe the way you felt as a genuine high? Of course that's what it felt like at the time, but looking back on it, how would it make you feel? Sick. Used. Abused. Betrayed.

Would you consider the "friend" generous, or fun, or kind any more? Of course you wouldn't; you'd see her for exactly what she is. It was money you simply couldn't afford, not an easy sum to write off and put down to experience.

I may have labored the analogy, but I make no apology. It perfectly describes your relationship with emotional eating. Anything remotely positive that you seemed to experience as a result of it was fake, phoney, and based on a confidence trick. A cruel combination of addiction and deception.

Does it matter that it's fake? Of course, it does.

CHANGING YOUR MINDSET

If the only reason you eat junk food is to relieve the low caused by the withdrawal from the previous fix and the release from having to exercise control, it seems reasonable to assume that all you need to do to get free is to stop eating junk food. Put up with the withdrawal for the short time it takes for the chemicals to pass out of your body and the craving will stop.

But we all know that this doesn't work. If it did, you would have quit by now without needing any help from me. The fly in the ointment is that while it may begin with something you put in your body, addiction lives and grows in the mind.

We've known for a long time that people can be brainwashed by bombarding them with propaganda. Evil dictators have used this technique with devastating effect throughout history. It's only recently, however, that we have begun to understand why we are susceptible to brainwashing.

Scientists have discovered that the brain is very plastic—meaning it can be literally molded and remolded by conditioning. Think of it as a network of electrical connections that fires off every time we have a thought, or process information, or pull something out of our memory. This network changes shape in order to give more capacity where it is needed and less where it is not.

If we are fed a lot of information on one particular subject, the network will remold itself to accommodate this information. This is how people become experts in specific fields; it's also how we become addicted.

The plasticity of the brain determines not only knowledge but attitude too. We call it mindset. The brainwashing we are bombarded with about junk food is designed to give us the mindset that junk food is a treat, a pleasure, a comfort.

OUR TASK IS TO CHANGE THAT MINDSET

Understanding this aspect of addiction enabled me to apply Easyway not only to smoking but to other recognized addictions such as alcoholism and heroin addiction, and also to addictions that don't involve recognized drugs, such as gambling and overeating. I'm happy to admit that I knew nothing of "brain plasticity" and "remolding" when I discovered the method, but as mentioned before, it's been interesting seeing science confirm the basis of Easyway.

You probably know a smoker who has quit but still craves cigarettes weeks, months, even years later. Some poor souls do so for the rest of their lives. This is because they have quit through sheer willpower alone. They haven't changed their mindset, so they continue to live with the illusion that smoking gave them a pleasure or comfort, and therefore they feel deprived. In their case, they never found out that the new friend was stealing from them and once their bank accounts had been stripped, the new friend disappeared into the night, never to be seen again. They're moping and mourning over something that was never real.

With all addictions, including emotional eating, we are brainwashed into believing that our little fix is a source of pleasure or comfort, and those moments of partial relief from withdrawal and control reinforce the illusion. Thus we are deluded into thinking that happiness lies in the very thing that's causing us misery.

Emotional eaters are lured to junk food by brainwashing. Once you've started trying to use food in an attempt to deal with emotions, it is the addiction to Bad Sugar and the illusion of pleasure that hooks you.

FILLING A VOID

It's helpful at this stage to understand exactly why we are drawn to things that we know to be "bad for us." It seems to go against the survival instinct that compels us to do things that are good for us. That's exactly what it is: When we're brainwashed, as we are by the junk food industry, our intellect overrides our instincts, convincing us that junk food is a pleasure or comfort DESPITE the fact that it can have a detrimental effect on our health.

In fact, the very fact that junk food is "bad" is part of its appeal. In the U.K., there was a famous advertising slogan for cream cakes:

"Naughty but nice." The real hook was not the word "nice"; it was "naughty."

We like the idea of being a bit naughty. It suggests personality, wit, nonconformity, individuality... It's an urge that is caused by an emptiness that opens up during our development, starting from birth. I call it "the void" and it affects all of us to different degrees.

The shock of birth leaves us desperately seeking security. We reach for our mothers and they protect us. Our neediness and vulnerability continues through childhood, when we're cocooned from the harsh realities of life in a world of carefree fun and make-believe. But before long, we reach the age where we discover that Santa Claus, the Easter Bunny and the Tooth Fairy don't exist.

At the same time, we're forced from the safety of home to school and a new set of fears and insecurities. We start to look more critically at our parents and it begins to dawn on us that they are not the unshakeable pillars of strength that we had always thought them to be. They have weaknesses, frailties, and fears, just as we do.

The disillusionment opens up a void in our minds, a feeling of emptiness and need. We fill the void with idols: pop stars, movie stars, TV celebrities, and sports players. We create our own fantasies. We idolize mere mortals and try to absorb some of their reflected glory. Instead of becoming complete, strong, secure, and unique individuals in our own right, we become followers, impressionable fans, leaving ourselves wide open to suggestion.

In the face of all this bewilderment and instability, we look for a little boost now and then. We've been brainwashed into believing that junk food will give us the comfort we need, that cigarettes and alcohol make you feel relaxed and happy, that gambling gives you a thrill. So we naturally turn to these things for relief from the void.

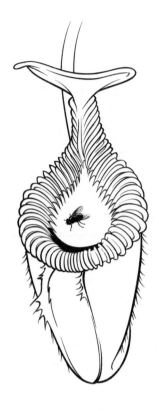

INGENIOUS BUT SIMPLE

The trap you are in is similar to a pitcher plant, a carnivorous plant shaped like a slender jug, which catches flies with an ingenious and cruel confidence trick. The fly lands on the rim of the plant, attracted by the sweet smell of its nectar. As it tucks into the nectar, it doesn't realize that it is being lured further into the plant. The nectar tastes like the best thing in the world, but it is the very thing that is luring the fly to its death.

Before we start seeking comfort in junk food, we're well aware of the negatives. We know that it can make us overweight and ruin our teeth. We probably know that it is a factor in obesity, high cholesterol, diabetes, and heart disease. Yet we also know that millions of people eat junk food quite regularly without apparently suffering any health problems.

We think our bodies will be able to cope. The body has an incredible ability to process junk—there was a man once who supposedly ate an entire airplane! Anyway, we don't intend to feel dependent on junk food. Nobody starts off with that intention. So we shelve our concerns about the harmful effects, tell ourselves we're in control and we can handle it, and focus on the apparent pleasure or comfort.

At the same time, the advertising industry bombards us with enticements to eat junk:

"**Naughty but nice**," "**We're lovin' it**," "**Finger lickin' good**,","**Helps you work, rest and play**," "**Gives you wiiings**," "**Have a break**."

These messages are accompanied by images of smiling, fit, healthy, happy people, luring you into the trap.

And so you take the plunge. You start eating junk and, guess what, nothing bad happens. So you do it again. But without realizing, you start to increase the quantity and frequency of your junk food consumption. Just as drug addicts increase the dose to get the same high, emotional eaters increase their eating…

YOU'RE ALREADY LOSING CONTROL

In the early days, you're able to con yourself that you remain in control of when and how much you eat and that there will be no problems. A chocolate bar once a day—what's the harm? But as time goes on and the pleasure or comfort you seek grows more and more elusive, you begin to sense that you're slipping further and further into a bottomless pit. It's an unhappy, insecure feeling that creates further anxiety and stress.

By now you've conditioned yourself to seek comfort from anxiety and stress by eating junk food. It feels like real comfort—like that friend who buys you all the drinks after work. So rather than dealing with the real cause of misery, you use the temporary fix of emotional eating.

You can see how this becomes a vicious circle of need, fix, withdrawal, need… And because you keep increasing the dose, the highs become more short-lived, the lows more intense, and the net effect is an increasingly rapid descent, like the fly sliding into the belly of the pitcher plant. This is how the trap works. It's how any addiction works.

EMOTIONAL EATERS SEEK COMFORT IN THE VERY
THING THAT'S CAUSING THEM MISERY

NATURE'S WARNING LIGHT

Pain, whether physical or emotional, serves a useful purpose: It tells us that something is wrong. The solution is to identify the cause of the problem and fix it. But we're conditioned by modern medicine to take a different approach. We treat the symptoms, not the cause. Have a headache? Take a painkiller. Feeling anxious? Pop a Xanax.

Imagine you're driving a car and the oil light comes on. What do you do? Stick tape over the light so you can no longer see it? Or pull over and top up the oil? Both actions will stop the oil light from flashing; but only one will prevent the engine from seizing up.

THE ADDICTION HAS TAKEN HOLD

As well as feeling that you're losing control of your eating, you notice the physical effects are starting to show. You're putting on weight, your skin is losing its glow, your hair is lank, you're getting out of breath more quickly... You try to cover up these signs and pretend they're not there, but these are ever-increasing, dark shadows looming at the back of your mind and as you slip further and further into the trap, they loom larger and larger, adding more and more to your misery.

You make repeated attempts to impose healthy eating regimes, fitness programs, constantly resolving to change, followed by failure.

Like the fly in the pitcher plant, you only realize you're trapped when you're well and truly hooked. But there is one crucial difference between the pitcher plant and the emotional-eating trap:

IT'S NEVER TOO LATE TO ESCAPE FROM
THE EMOTIONAL EATING TRAP

Unlike the fly, you're not standing on a slippery slope; there is no physical force compelling you to eat more. The trap is entirely in your mind. Ingeniously it makes you your own jailer, so the more you struggle, the tighter the bonds become, but fortunately for you that is also its fatal weakness. You have the power to set yourself free simply by following the instructions in this book.

Further good news is that you recover completely when you stop. Without the mental and physical lows induced by emotional eating, you will be able to get back to par and start seeing the occasional low as a natural part of life, not something you need to relieve with junk food.

Remember too that the fact that you've fallen into the trap has nothing to do with your character or personality. Millions of people, who have found themselves in the same trap and been convinced that they will never be able to escape, have gotten free and so will you.

SO WHAT'S HOLDING YOU BACK?

There are two major myths keeping you in the trap:

1. The myth that junk food gives you pleasure and/or comfort.

2. The myth that quitting will be hard and miserable.

As long as you believe these two common myths, you'll find it hard to quit emotional eating. No matter how much you *want* to quit, part of your brain will be telling you you'll be happier if you don't. You need to change your mindset and that means unraveling these myths.

We are conned into believing that junk food gives pleasure and comfort by the junk food industry and its advertising agents. As I will explain later in the book, there is no genuine pleasure or comfort to be gained from eating junk food. There is plenty of misery and discomfort, as you've discovered.

But part of your brain will still be telling you that emotional eating is a source of pleasure or comfort for you and, in spite of the "new friend" analogy, you might still be thinking, "Does it matter that it isn't true if it feels like it is?"

There are two very strong arguments that should answer that question once and for all.

1. Emotional eating is a threat to your physical and mental health and there's only so long you can go on burying your head in the sand before these grim realities begin to take a very heavy toll.

2. If you were happy about emotional eating, you wouldn't be reading this book.

Sooner or later, all addicts realize that there is no pleasure or comfort in their addiction. By this stage they are like the fly, descending rapidly into the belly of the pitcher plant. There is a point at which the fly senses that all is not well and thinks about flying out. It's nearly always too late. The fly struggles a bit, loses its footing and falls into the digestive juices.

For you, though, there is no physical force preventing your escape. So when you sense that you are being consumed by emotional eating and want to get free, you are in a very strong position to do so. You know there is no pleasure, no comfort, no reason at all to keep eating junk. From here it is a short step to establishing the mindset you need to walk free.

It's harder for people who still have the illusion of pleasure to change their mindset. Once the illusion of pleasure is gone, there is only one thing holding you back: Fear.

It's a strange kind of fear: The fear that escaping the misery of emotional eating will leave you in a more miserable place. But it's a very real fear and we will tackle it very soon. First, though, we need to look more closely at the illusion of pleasure and the false beliefs that keep it alive in your mind.

Chapter 6

BUYING THE CON

IN THIS CHAPTER

• INTELLECT v. INSTINCT • HOW TO SPOT THE TRUTH
• IT MAKES ME HAPPY • I CAN HANDLE IT • IT'S THE WAY I'M MADE

People who don't have the eating problem you do find it hard to understand why you can't just stop. What they don't realize is that the trap is a web of illusions that makes it impossible to see the way out. Easyway enables your escape by helping you to see through those illusions.

Among the negative feelings suffered by emotional eaters is a feeling of foolishness. "How can I be so crazy as to keep eating this stuff when I know it's making me miserable?" For creatures as sophisticated and intelligent as humans, it does seem incredible that we can be so easily duped into self-destruction. And remember, it's not just you who has been taken in by these illusions; millions of people have fallen for the same con.

I mentioned in Chapter 2 that the key difference between human beings and wild animals is that animals survive solely by instinct. We also use instinct to survive—it tells us when and what to eat; it alerts us to danger; it helps us to find a suitable mate—but we don't rely on instinct alone. We use our intellect to give us power over the whole animal kingdom.

INTELLECT v. INSTINCT

Intellect has enabled us to learn and pass on our learning, with the result that we have developed into a highly sophisticated species that is not only capable of building fantastic structures and machines but also has an appreciation of art, music, romance, spirituality, and so on.

Intellect is a wonderful thing, but it can go to your head: We tend to respect intellectual behavior above instinctive behavior and this is what has led us astray. Instinct is Mother Nature's survival kit, but when it conflicts with our intellect, we usually take the intellectual option.

WE THINK WE CAN OUTSMART THE SURVIVAL INSTINCT

A stark example is the sportsman who needs a pain-killing injection in order to play. His instincts are giving the clear signal to rest and allow the injury to recover, but his intellect tells him he can numb the pain and play on. The result is irreversible damage to his body. His instinct was right, yet he chose to side with his intellect.

Look again at the "advances" the human race has made and you'll see that, rather than building on the advantage that Mother Nature has given us, we have devoted a remarkable amount of time to self-destruction. We have devised, and continue to devise, ever more sophisticated ways of killing each other in battle, but it's not just when we're trying to be destructive that our intellect leads us astray. It's also evident in the food we eat.

By allowing our intellect to trick our instincts, we have become a species of compulsive junk food consumers. Refined sugar is a prime example. The reason we are so partial to refined sugar, and all the candy, cakes, and drinks that contain it, is that it replicates the natural sugar we derive from fruit.

Fruit is the food that nature designed for us to eat. It is packed with nutrients and is easy to eat and digest. Our taste for the natural sugars in fruit is designed to keep us coming back for more. Refined sugar contains none of the goodness of fruit, yet it tricks our taste buds into thinking it's the same thing. Intellectually we have created a substance that fools our instincts into thinking we are getting something good when, in truth, it is nothing but bad.

And I mean that: there is ABSOLUTELY NO GOODNESS WHATSOEVER in refined sugar.

A lot of the intellectual choices we make in life are beneficial. For example, intellect enables us to forecast and preempt problems in a way that other animals can't, and thus to protect ourselves better. But choosing to eat junk food is not beneficial. So why make that choice?

The reason is…

WE DON'T ALWAYS REALIZE WE HAVE AN OPTION

Of course, eating junk food is a choice. Nobody is holding a gun to your head and forcing you to eat it. But the brainwashing is so strong and the illusions it creates so convincing that it doesn't occur to you that you have a choice.

There are a lot of people who stand to gain by conning you into eating junk food. The manufacturers, the retailers, the advertisers… It is in their interests to find ways to convince you into making that intellectual decision. And they have become masters at it. Your intellect is their greatest asset, allowing them to fill your head with false information that overrides your instincts and fools you into believing the two myths:

1. The myth that eating junk food gives you pleasure and/or comfort.

2. The myth that quitting is hard and miserable.

HOW TO SPOT THE TRUTH

It's not hard to trick the human mind. Remember the picture of men in Chapter 2. This is a visual example of how easy it is to sow false information in your mind. But it also illustrates the fact that once you've seen through an illusion, you can't be fooled by it again.

This brings me to a question that a lot of people ask of Easyway:

HOW DO I KNOW THAT EASYWAY IS NOT JUST BRAINWASHING ME IN A DIFFERENT WAY?

The way addictions work is to bombard your mental process with a false sense of pleasure and reward, which your mind comes to mistake for the real thing. Your instinct has been reprogrammed into believing that you need to eat junk in order to get the pleasure or comfort you need. At the same time, your intellect has been fed the same misinformation. As long as you continue to believe that junk food gives you pleasure or comfort, you will not be able to reprogram your instinct to distinguish this false reward from the real thing.

Easyway does the opposite to brainwashing; it's actually COUNTER-BRAINWASHING. It helps you to see through the illusions and unravel the myths that hold you back from walking free.

The first illusion is the one that most of us are taken in by:

"I ENJOY THE TASTE"

From an early age we are led to believe that there is something special about sweet things. The act of denying these foods to a child only reinforces that impression. "You can't have your ice cream until you've eaten your sandwiches." Of course we're going to regard ice cream as the special treat.

We grow up believing that sugary foods taste delicious. But if your reason for eating these junk foods was the taste, wouldn't it make sense not to swallow them? You could get the flavor by chewing them and spitting them out and you wouldn't have to take all the badness down into your stomach.

In truth, we don't savor these foods at all. We wolf them down, and there can only be one reason for that: Because we want to get our fix as quickly as possible. It's not genuine pleasure that drives us to eat these foods; it's the *idea* of pleasure. We don't eat them for the taste; we eat them for the sugar and the effect it has on our brain and body.

Remember the last time you binged on cookies or ice cream or chocolate. Did you take your time, carefully tasting it, savoring every morsel? Or did you consume it in a frenzy of guilt?

No doubt you wished to stretch it out to make it last, but in truth unless you deliberately exercise huge control to do so, you wolfed it down in no time.

Next time you eat a cake or chocolate bar or whatever, pay attention to the way you eat it.

Slow down, chew the food, and be aware of the taste and feel of it in your mouth. You will become increasingly aware that it's a dry lump of stodge.

Most junk food tastes of very little at all. Most desserts are flavored with fruit to make them taste of something. But it's not the taste that keeps you coming back for more; it's the sugar addiction.

IT MAKES ME HAPPY

Even in the depths of despair, some emotional eaters continue to regard junk food as the one thing that can make them happy. It never dawns on them that it is the cause of their misery.

We are brainwashed into believing that sugary foods will make us happy by both the advertisers and by one another. We reinforce the illusion by giving each other gifts of chocolates, celebrating with cake, rewarding with cookies.

Chocolate is an ingenious example of brainwashing. It is made of three basic ingredients: cocoa, which tastes foul if eaten unsweetened and contains an addictive drug called theobromine, which is related to caffeine; refined sugar to disguise the foul taste; and cow's milk, which was intended to nourish calves, to improve its appearance. Each component is harmful to the human body in its own way, yet when they're put together they form a product that has an enchanting effect, fooling us into believing that we are eating something wonderful.

The brainwashing has been so effective that we regard chocolate as a flavor, and use it to make other junk foods more appealing. There is a growing misconception that chocolate is something natural and wholesome. It's true that some chocolate is more processed and contains more junk than other items, but there is no such thing as "pure" chocolate. It is all processed and contains the addictive theobromine.

We are brainwashed into believing that chocolate, candy, cakes, and other sugary foods help social occasions go with a swing. We allow ourselves to be convinced that they comfort us when we're lonely, stressed, or sad.

It's easy to be fooled. If you've ever been out on a sunny day and passed a grocery store and thought, "I'd love a bag of potato chips," you'll know what a lovely feeling it is walking down the street eating that bag of your favorite flavor. It's an experience that will stay with you and reinforce the belief that the chips made you happy. But the truth is you would have been happy anyway. It wasn't the potato chips that made you happy; it was the circumstances in which you were eating them.

Comfort eating is a misnomer. The idea that stuffing a lump of stodge down your throat somehow gives you comfort is hard to swallow (I make no apology for the pun). If you have understood my explanation of addiction, you will know that the illusion of comfort is merely the relief of discomfort, which was caused by eating junk food in the first place.

All emotional eaters know that eating junk food to make you happy doesn't work. Whatever it is that is causing you to feel unhappy, eating sugary foods that contain no nutritional benefits at all will not help. All it will do is partially relieve the low caused by the previous fix of junk. The feeling of sadness, loneliness, anxiety, or whatever remains. Add the discomfort and self-loathing that come with overeating and you will end up more unhappy than when you started.

Emotional eaters kid themselves that they enjoy gorging on junk food because the alternative is too awful to contemplate. If you admit that you don't enjoy it, that means facing up to the fact that you are not in control and continue to eat junk only because you can't resist the temptation.

You have a choice. Accept the truth and follow the instructions to escape, or keep on lying to protect yourself from the pathetic truth: that emotional eating is causing you untold harm but you are helpless to stop.

TAKE YOUR HEAD OUT OF THE SAND!

Remember, the reason emotional eaters go on believing they get some pleasure or comfort from eating junk is because when they are not eating, they feel restless and uncomfortable. When they eat, the uncomfortable feeling is partially relieved. It feels like a boost, but it is only making them feel like a nonaddict feels all the time.

IT'S LIKE DELIBERATELY WEARING TIGHT SHOES JUST FOR THE PLEASURE OF TAKING THEM OFF!

I CAN HANDLE IT

Aside from the fact that this is a bizarre reason for choosing to eat anything, the evidence is that you can't handle it.

We are warned from an early age that sugary foods are bad for our teeth, make us fat, give us spots, and lead to other problems. Yet we grow up thinking we'll be OK: We can brush our teeth, take some exercise, use skincare products. No one talks about the threat of addiction and the misery that can cause.

We regard junk food as a guilty pleasure, nothing more sinister than that. But you know very well how it can tangle you up in its trap and keep you hooked, even though you wish you could stop. By the time you understand the real danger of junk food, it's too late and you're well and truly stuck. The good news is that it's never too late to get out. Once you've seen the truth, it's easy to dispel the illusion that eating junk food is a relatively harmless habit.

IT'S THE WAY I'M MADE

Addicts of all kinds often put their addiction down to a flaw in their personality. It's either a weakness in their temperament, a lack of willpower or—because of a predisposition to addiction—an addictive personality. The implication in both cases is that the situation is beyond their control, an excuse that suits addicts very well because it removes the pressure to stop.

If this sounds absurd, that's because addiction is absurd. It drives us to make absurd decisions and to behave in absurd ways. Addicts know that their addiction is destructive and desperately wish they could quit, yet they lie and make excuses and try every trick in the book to make sure they can carry on.

The problem is that the bulk of information we receive about addictions is that you *do* need willpower to quit and that there *is* such a thing as an addictive personality. The fact that this misinformation is put about by many reputable organizations that exist to help addicts only adds to its potency.

Why would an organization that genuinely wants to help people put out information that serves to imprison them more deeply in the trap? The simple answer is because they too have been brainwashed and have never stopped to look at the situation another way.

The absurdity of addiction is the reason why I ask you to keep an open mind and follow the instructions: Because the truth is often the exact opposite of what we assume to be true.

The belief that your eating problem is down to a flaw in your personality is a form of denial.

Rather than accepting that you have an addiction and taking the necessary steps to overcome it, this enables you to say, "I have no choice but to carry on doing it."

But why would anyone want to say that? Why would anyone who is suffering the misery and slavery of emotional eating make an excuse that took away their option to walk free?

The answer can be encapsulated in one word, which lies at the root of all addictions:

FEAR

Chapter 7

FEAR

IN THIS CHAPTER

• *A TUG-OF-WAR* • *PROJECTED FEARS* • *FEAR OF FAILURE*
• *FEAR OF SUCCESS* • *WIN THE TUG-OF-WAR* • *REMOVE ALL DOUBTS*

Fear of the consequences of emotional eating is what drives you to try and quit, but there are other fears pulling in the opposite direction. Let's see if we can help you dispel all your fears.

All addicts make excuses. Emotional eaters have to make excuses because they know there is no logical reason to keep gorging themselves on junk. So what do you tell yourself?

"I'm not feeling very strong today. Tomorrow will be different."

"I've eaten most of the package, I might as well finish it off."

You need excuses to go on eating junk because you're afraid of what might happen if you try to quit. You have been brainwashed into thinking that you derive some pleasure or comfort from it, and so the thought of life without it is scary. At the same time, you're aware of the harm you're inflicting on yourself and you're afraid of the long-term damage.

You're caught in a tug-of-war between conflicting fears and it makes you think contradictory thoughts:

"I know it's making me miserable, but it's my one pleasure in life."

I don't need to point out to you that…

SOMETHING THAT MAKES YOU MISERABLE CANNOT BE A PLEASURE

PROJECTED FEARS

Fear is nothing to be ashamed of. It's a hugely powerful emotion and one that's crucial to our survival. It's interesting because it can be both instinctive and intellectual. It is the instinct that drives us to fight or flight, alerting us to danger and making us wary in potentially dangerous situations. But the things that frighten us can be both real and imaginary. An amusement park ride, a horror film: We know how to create fear without real danger; the suggestion of danger is enough to trigger the instinct of fear.

We can imagine danger, even where there is none. This is both an asset and a handicap. Our ability to learn about potential dangers also helps us to avoid them. The fears associated with losing your job, for example, are intellectual. You have learned about the possible consequences of finding yourself unemployed—for example, having no money, being forced to sell your possessions, sacrificing the pleasures and comforts that you enjoy now, feeling worthless and unfulfilled – and so you do everything in your power to safeguard your job and make yourself indispensable, even when there is no present threat of losing your job.

In this case, your intellect does you a good service. But what if your projected fears are based on false information? You can be made fearful of dangers that don't exist too—like the fear of life without junk food.

There is absolutely nothing to fear from NOT eating junk food, and from a physical health perspective we all know this very well, yet you've been brainwashed into believing that life without your regular fix will be uncomfortable and miserable. As consumers, we are bombarded with so much false information that it's impossible for us to know what to believe. We end up spending a lot of our life worrying about things that will never happen—and being blasé about things that will.

Fear is the basis of all addiction. It is the force that makes the trap so ingenious, convincing the addict that there is some kind of pleasure or comfort in the trap. It is ingenious because it works back to front. It's when you are not eating that you suffer the empty, insecure feeling. When you eat, you feel a small boost, which partially relieves the insecure feeling and your brain is fooled into believing that eating junk is providing a comfort.

This is why, as an emotional eater, you cannot find true happiness while you remain in the trap. When you're eating junk, you'll wish you didn't have to. When you can't eat it, you'll wish you could.

> ***ONCE YOU UNDERSTAND THE TRAP COMPLETELY, YOU
> WILL HAVE NO MORE NEED OR DESIRE TO EAT JUNK***

FEAR OF FAILURE

Being an emotional eater is like being in a prison. Every aspect of your life is controlled by eating: your daily routine, your hopes, your view of the world, your suffering. Of course, you're not physically imprisoned. There are no walls or bars. The prison is purely in your mind, but as long as you remain a slave to junk food, you will experience the same psychological symptoms as an inmate in a physical prison.

If you've tried and failed to conquer your emotional eating problem, you'll know that it leaves you feeling more firmly trapped than you did before you tried. It's like that moment in a movie when a prisoner is thrown into a cell and the first thing he does is run to the door and tug at the handle. This confirms his predicament: He really is locked in.

Trying and failing to quit eating junk has the same effect. It reinforces the belief that you are trapped in a prison from which there is no escape. This can be a crushing experience and it's quite natural to make your mind up that the best way to avoid the misery of failure is to avoid trying in the first place.

The twisted logic of addiction concludes that as long as you never try to escape, you will always be able to preserve the belief that escape is possible. It is only when you try to escape that it becomes impossible.

When it's written down like this you can see how absurd this thinking is, and yet it's not so clear when you're the one caught in the trap. The belief that escape is possible is very important to an addict. It represents hope. And who wants to risk shattering their own hope?

There are millions of intelligent people around the world who continue to keep themselves trapped in this way. They prefer to continue suffering the misery of addiction than risk the misery of failure. What they don't realize—and it's never pointed out to them until they discover Easyway—is that the person who tugs at the prison door and finds it firmly locked is using the wrong method of escape.

Tugging at the door is the equivalent of using the willpower method. The trap is like a snare, which tightens its grip the more you struggle. This is why it's often people with very strong willpower who find it hardest to quit.

The fear of trying and failing to quit is illogical. The thing you're fearing has already happened. You've become addicted. What could be worse? Every time you fall for the temptation to eat a cake or chocolate bar, you experience the sense of failure. As long as you remain an addict, you will continue to feel a failure. Perhaps you're afraid that trying and failing to quit will only increase your sense of failure. I can assure you it won't—not if you follow the correct method.

When channelled properly, the fear of failure can be a positive force. It's the emotion that focuses the mind of the runner on the starting blocks, the ballerina waiting in the wings, the student going into an exam. Fear of failure is the little voice in your head that reminds you to prepare thoroughly, to remember everything you've rehearsed and trained for, and to leave nothing to chance. It can bring a remarkable clarity of thought and judgement.

But the addict's fear of failure is based on an illusion. The truth is you have nothing to lose by trying, even if you fail. The worst that can happen is that you remain in the trap. By not trying, you guarantee that outcome. In other words:

IF YOU SUCCUMB TO THE FEAR OF FAILURE, YOU ARE GUARANTEED TO SUFFER THE VERY THING YOU FEAR

But there is another fear we have to come to terms with before you can make your escape.

FEAR OF SUCCESS

Many studies have been carried out into the psychological effects on prison inmates and ex-prisoners. One phenomenon that repeats with depressing regularity is the tendency for released prisoners to reoffend within a very short period after being let out. You might assume that these are habitual criminals who aren't very smart, but research has shown that in many cases ex-cons reoffend deliberately to get caught. They actually *want* to go back inside.

Prison life is grim. But when it's the life you know, it can be more attractive than the alternative... or less frightening anyway. Life on the outside is alien and disconcerting. It's not what you know. You don't feel equipped to handle it. You yearn for the "security" of the prison.

This is very similar to the psychology of addiction. Addicts are afraid that life without their "crutch" will feel insecure and disconcerting. They won't be able to enjoy life or cope with its stresses; they might even have to go through some terrible trauma to get free and then they'll be condemned to a life of sacrifice and deprivation.

We are all led to believe that life without "naughty" treats is no fun. For emotional eaters, this belief becomes the monster that keeps you in the trap. Though you're well aware of the misery that your eating causes, you may now have come to regard it as part of your identity. Perhaps you've even convinced yourself that people like you because of it.

We see it time and time again in the media: The "foodaholic" who doesn't seem to care, who isn't tied down by those petty concerns that make everyone else so uptight and boring. They're portrayed as being more fun, more grounded, more lovable. Perhaps you believe in this portrayal. Perhaps you believe that this person is you. But ask yourself:

• Do you feel grounded?

• Do you feel lovable?

• Are you really having fun?

Be absolutely clear about this: You have nothing to lose by escaping the emotional eating trap. Life without the slavery of addiction is not something to fear; it is something to look forward to with excitement and elation. Choose to stay in the trap and you will feel a failure for the rest of your life. This is NOT the life you were born for. You have a choice.

WIN THE TUG-OF-WAR

The trap makes you your own jailer and this is both its fiendish ingenuity and its fatal flaw. The panic feeling that makes you afraid to even try to quit eating junk is caused by eating junk. One of the greatest benefits you'll receive when you quit is never suffering that fear again.

The tug-of-war is a conflict between two fears: The fear of what your eating problem is doing to you and the fear of life without your little "crutch." One of these fears is valid because it's based on fact; the other is invalid because it's based on illusions. But the tug-of-war is easy to win because both fears are caused by the same thing: Eating junk.

TAKE AWAY THE JUNK AND THE FEAR GOES TOO

If I could transport you now into your mind and body by the time you have finished reading this book, you would think, "Wow! Do I really feel this good?" Fear will have been replaced by elation, the feeling of failure by optimism, self-loathing by confidence, apathy by dynamism. As a result of these psychological turnarounds, your physical health will improve too. You'll look healthier and you'll enjoy both a newfound energy and the ability to truly relax.

Some people manage to go for weeks, months, even years without succumbing to the temptation to eat junk but still find that they miss it. You may have been through this yourself. This method is different. Believe me, you will not miss it because you are not giving anything up. There is no sacrifice involved because junk food does nothing for you whatsoever.

All you are doing is removing something from your life that makes you miserable and replacing it with something that makes you genuinely happy.

It's nothing more difficult than throwing away a pair of tight shoes and replacing them with a comfortable new pair.

YOU ARE NOT GIVING ANYTHING UP

You are trading the constant battle for control and loss of control over your eating for total control; more accurately, you're trading no choice for absolute choice. You don't need to exercise control or willpower to eat naturally and healthily.

Right now, part of you feels that junk food is your friend, your constant companion, and comfort. Get it clear in your mind that this is an illusion. In reality, junk food is your worst enemy and, far from supporting you, it's driving you deeper and deeper into despair. You instinctively know this, so open your mind and follow your instincts.

REMOVE ALL DOUBTS

Take a moment to think about all the good things you stand to gain by overcoming your emotional eating problem. Think of the enormous self-respect you'll have, the time and energy you'll save by not having to make excuses and cover up your eating habits.

That phoney little boost you feel every time you get your fix of junk food is a mere hint of how you will feel all the time when you're free…

WHEN YOU'RE FREE, IT'S REAL

The difficulty for all addicts is being able to step outside their world and see their problem as other people see it. If you saw a heroin addict suffering the misery of drug addiction, would you advise them to keep injecting heroin into their veins, rather than try living without that high they seem to get every time they get a fix? If you can see that the "high" is nothing more than relief from the terrible craving that is caused by the drug as it leaves the body, you are well on the way to understanding your own addiction. And it should be clear to you that there is only one way to stop your craving…

STOP EATING JUNK!

It's as simple as that. Once you can see that there is nothing to fear, that you are not giving up anything or depriving yourself in any way, stopping is easy.

So far I've given you three instructions to put you in the right frame of mind, so that this book can help you overcome your emotional eating problem:

1. Follow all the instructions

2. Keep an open mind

3. Begin with a feeling of elation

If you are struggling with any of these instructions, go back and re-read the relevant chapters. It's essential that you don't just follow the instructions but that you understand them.

We have established that eating junk food does absolutely nothing positive for you whatsoever, that the beliefs that have imprisoned you in the trap are merely illusions, and that you have everything to gain and nothing to lose by quitting. Are we agreed, therefore, that there is nothing to fear? If you are in agreement, then you're ready to move on.

If you're afraid that the process itself will be unpleasant, perhaps because you've tried to quit before and found it a torturing experience, remember that the willpower method doesn't work. It leaves you feeling deprived, which means you can never truly rid yourself of the desire to fall back into the trap. This method is different.

Before you're ready to move on, you need to be sure that you have removed the fear of success and the fear of failure. You need to be 100 percent certain about your desire to quit. If you have any doubts, please go back and reread this chapter, paying special attention to the arguments that prove that both fears have no logical basis.

The fourth instruction is this:

NEVER DOUBT YOUR DECISION TO QUIT

As we go through the book, you will be challenged to see things in a new way and this may cause you some doubts. It's absolutely fine to question what you read because that will help to reinforce the logic and truth behind it.

But if you find yourself doubting your decision to quit, remind yourself why you chose to read this book in the first place and think about all the wonderful gains you stand to make.

If you're resolute about your desire to quit but still have doubts about your ability to do so, that's probably because you're not convinced that it's possible to quit without willpower. It's time we addressed this particular myth once and for all.

Chapter 8

WILLPOWER

IN THIS CHAPTER

• *THE WRONG METHOD* • *HOW WEAK-WILLED ARE YOU?*
• *A NEVER-ENDING STRUGGLE* • *CROSSING THE LINE THE EASY WAY*
• *OTHER QUITTERS*

Determination is a wonderful thing. It gives us the resolve to accomplish all sorts of incredible feats, driving us on when we feel like giving up. But addiction is not a mountain to be conquered; it is a figment of your imagination. You don't need willpower to see the truth; you just need an open mind.

Easyway can help you overcome the addiction of emotional eating without any pain or sacrifice and, therefore, without the need for willpower. A common response to this claim is, "If it's so easy, why do so many people find it incredibly hard?" The reason is simple: They are using the wrong method.

The simplest of tasks can become virtually impossible if you go about them the wrong way. Think about opening a door. You know how to open a door—you push on the handle and it swings open with minimal effort. But have you ever come across a door with no handle and pushed on the wrong side, where the hinges are? You're met with instant resistance. The door might budge a tiny bit, but it won't swing open. It requires a huge amount of effort and determination to open it far enough for you to walk through. Of course, you don't keep pushing on the wrong side; you change your method, pushing on the correct side, and the door opens so easily you barely pay it any notice.

THE WRONG METHOD

Overcoming addiction is just like opening a door. Use the wrong method and it's incredibly hard; use the right method and it's easy.

Most emotional eaters find it difficult to stop because they try to use willpower to overcome their desire to eat junk. They have a constant conflict of will, a mental tug-of-war. On one side, their rational brain knows they should stop because it's detrimental to their health, appearance, self-esteem, and happiness. On the other side, their addicted brain makes them panic at the thought of being deprived of their pleasure or comfort.

When you try to quit with the willpower method, you set yourself up for a series of setbacks. You begin by focusing on all the reasons for stopping and have to hope your will is strong enough to hold out until the desire eventually goes.

This seems logical, but there's a problem: You still regard junk food as a pleasure or comfort; therefore, when you stop eating it, you feel you're making a sacrifice. This makes you miserable. It also makes you feel you deserve a reward. Now, what have you always done when you need cheering up or you deserve a reward?

THE WILLPOWER METHOD MAKES YOU MORE HOOKED THAN EVER

You only need willpower to stop if you have a conflict of will. We are going to resolve that conflict by removing one side of the tug-of-war, so that you have no desire to eat junk. Using willpower for the rest of your life to try not to eat junk is unlikely to prove successful and will not make you happy; removing the need and desire to eat junk will.

Some people do manage to stop their addictive behavior through sheer force of will, but do they ever actually break free of their addiction? There are people who quit for years and then fall back into the trap. We hear from lots of them. Despite having quit for so long that their addiction is a distant memory, they still believe that junk food is a pleasure or comfort, so they haven't removed the desire and sense of sacrifice. All it takes is something to trigger their need for a pick-me-up or reward and they turn to their old fix. Their will fails and they end up back in the trap, feeling more miserable than before.

HOW WEAK-WILLED ARE YOU?

Just as people generally assume that quitting requires willpower, those who fail to quit are assumed to be weak-willed. Indeed, emotional eaters typically criticize themselves for being weak-willed. If you think you've been unable to control your emotional eating up until now because you lack the strength of will, you haven't yet understood the nature of the trap you're in.

Strong-willed people actually find it harder to quit because they refuse to open their mind and accept they're using the wrong method. They would rather grapple with the problem than accept that they've been brainwashed and are not in control. The nature of the trap is such that the more you fight it, the more tightly ensnared you become.

FAILURE TO QUIT IS MORE LIKELY TO BE A SIGN
OF A STRONG WILL THAN A WEAK ONE

A NEVER-ENDING STRUGGLE

Ask yourself whether you're weak-willed in other ways. Perhaps you're a smoker or you drink too much, and you regard these conditions as further evidence of a weak will. There is indeed a connection between all addictions, but the connection is not that they are signs of a lack of willpower. On the contrary, they are more likely evidence of a strong will. What they all share is that they are traps created by misleading information and untruths. And one of the most misleading untruths is that quitting requires willpower—because when you think something is going to be hard and unpleasant, you find excuses not to try.

IN HER OWN WORDS: MEL

I came to the U.S.A. in my early 20s and set up a business, which did very well. I worked incredibly hard and frequently had to overcome huge hurdles faced by anyone running a business. There were countless occasions when I came close to throwing in the towel, but I didn't let myself. I dug in and pulled through.

Part of my success was down to my ability to get on with people and build relationships and a big part of that was taking them out for lunch and dinner. In those circumstances, it's hard not to overindulge. I started putting on weight and I hated it. I told myself I'd join a gym, but I never found the time.

Worse than that, I was actually turning to food to cheer myself up. I would come back from some fancy lunch, feeling bloated and sluggish, but then when it was time for my afternoon break I'd go out and buy a cake. I couldn't resist it.

It was like I was permanently hungry, though if I'd stopped to think about how I really felt I would have realized that I was *never* hungry. I never went without food for long enough.

There was always a voice in my head saying, "Go on, you've earned it."

I couldn't understand why, despite the misery I felt every time I looked in the mirror, I couldn't motivate myself to do anything about it. I was used to being in control, but here was something that seemed to have me completely wrapped up in its clutches. I felt utterly helpless. And that made me utterly depressed.

Splitting up with my boyfriend was the catalyst for deciding to quit. I made my mind up I had to lose 50 pounds. I hired a personal trainer and forbade myself to eat anything sugary. I worked hard and after three months I had succeeded in losing 50 pounds. But it had not been easy. In fact, I would say it was hell. But I did it and my first thought, as I climbed off the scales beaming, was, "Go on, girl, you deserve it." I celebrated with a cream cake and a bottle of wine. And guess what? Within three months, I'd put all the weight back on.

It takes a strong-willed person to persist in doing something that goes against all their instincts. You know that eating junk is having an increasingly bad effect on your body, as well as making you emotionally stressed and unhappy and distracting you from the things you do well, leaving you feeling worthless and helpless—yet you keep finding excuses for doing it. That is not the behavior of a weak-willed person.

When you go to the lengths emotional eaters do to cover up their addiction: Sneaking off to go shopping, hiding food in drawers, appearing to diet in public but gorging in private... all these actions take a lot of planning and a strong will.

If I saw you trying to open a door by pushing on the hinges and I told you you'd find it easier if you pushed on the handle, but you ignored me and insisted on pushing on the hinges, I'd call you wilful, not weak-willed. The prisoner who reoffends soon after being released from prison is not weak-willed; he is displaying a strong will to get back inside.

Think of all the people you know who have an eating problem. It's probably a small list because nobody likes to admit to it. But there are enough high-profile examples to illustrate the fact that emotional eating is not exclusive to the weak-willed.

You'll be familiar with the expression "fat cat." The overweight company boss is a classic stereotype. From Roman emperors to high-flying bankers, we associate overeating with success. Of course, there's a direct correlation between wealth and the amount you can afford to spend on food, but having money doesn't automatically mean you go and spend it on having more food than you need, and they are so busy looking looking after the challenges of their lives they forget to look after themselves.

If a high-flyer has a weight problem, it'll be because he or she regards junk food as a pleasure or comfort. Fat cats spend so much time fighting battles and overcoming challenges that it's exhausting. They comfort and reward themselves with junk food and alcohol.

Every so often they'll force themselves through a strict diet and exercise regime, lose a few pounds, feel they've gotten things back under control and go straight back to their old behaviors. Ballooning up and down like this might seem like a weakness, but these people are not weak-willed.

Everything else about their life shows that they are extremely strong-willed, so there must be something else preventing them from taking control of their eating, something other than willpower (or lack of it).

I'm sure you too can find evidence that you are strong-willed. How do you react when people tell you you shouldn't eat this or that? Don't you find you tend to do the opposite?

Wouldn't you describe that as wilful?

It tends to be the most strong-willed people who find it hardest to quit by using the willpower method because when the door fails to open, they won't give up and try to find an easier method; they'll force themselves to keep pushing on the hinges until they can push no more.

IN HIS OWN WORDS: NICK

I managed to stop eating cakes, chocolate and candy for a whole year once. I made my mind up on New Year's Eve and I stuck to my guns until the following New Year's celebrations. I avoided cake shops, candy stores, the dessert aisle in the supermarket. I never looked at the dessert options in restaurants. I had real determination when I started and it was quite easy because lots of my friends were abstaining from certain foods and booze for January. I thought, "Great! This is going to be a breeze."

But as the weeks went by, I found that I was still having to draw on all my willpower to resist the temptations that came my way. In fact, it seemed to be getting harder. I had expected to lose all desire for junk food once I'd gone without it for a month or so, but that wasn't the case. I was constantly having to avoid places where I thought I might be tempted and I could feel myself wanting to cave in.

When Christmas came, I redoubled my efforts and made it through without any chocolate, pies, cake, anything. I thought I'd done really well. But on New Year's Eve it all came tumbling down. I started tucking in to the desserts and felt this wave of relief, until I was horribly sick at the end of the night.

I woke up hating myself. I knew I'd blown a year's worth of hard work and it hit me hard. The worst thing was that I felt I'd come really close to making it. I'd told myself that if I could get through to January, I'd be able to say I was cured. But I'd fallen just short.

I lost all self-respect and started eating to punish myself. I almost reveled in piling the weight back on—the man who had blown it just short of the finish line; I didn't think I deserved any better.

I now understand that my attempt was doomed to failure from the start. When I thought I was close to the finish line I was really nowhere near. With the willpower method, there is no finish line.

When you try to quit by the willpower method, the struggle never ends. As long as you continue to believe that you're giving something up, you'll always be running in pain. The stronger your will, the longer you will withstand the agony. Nick was strong-willed enough to hold out for a whole year, but the pain only got worse because the longer he went on feeling deprived, the more powerful his craving became.

CROSSING THE LINE THE EASY WAY

With Easyway, there is a finish line and you don't have to wait months or years to cross it. With Easyway, you cross the finish line as soon as you remove the fear and illusions and lose the desire to eat junk. That's when you are free of the addiction that has turned you into an emotional eater. You need to understand that you will not get to that line by forcing yourself to suffer.

Addicts do not respond well to a hard-line approach. Rather than helping you to quit, the willpower method actually encourages you to stay hooked because...

1. It reinforces the myth that quitting is hard and, therefore, adds to your fear.

2. It creates a feeling of deprivation, which you will seek to alleviate in your usual way—you will fall back into the trap.

Once you have failed using the willpower method, it's even harder to try again because you will have reinforced the belief that you have a problem that is impossible to cure.

People like Nick, who have tried the willpower method and failed, will tell you they felt an enormous sense of relief when they first gave in. It's important to understand that this relief is nothing more than a temporary end to the self-inflicted pain.

It's not relief that makes you feel happy. No one celebrates falling back into the trap. Nick woke up hating himself. This is a common experience among emotional eaters.

That first fix after you've tried to quit is not pleasurable at all despite what others might tell you. They're confusing pleasure with the relief of ending their pain. It's nothing more than the feeling of relief you get when you take off a pair of tight shoes at the end of the day.

OTHER QUITTERS

From time to time you come across people who are trying to improve their diet and lose weight by using willpower. You probably admire their determination and wish you could do the same. Think again!

Remember what you have learned about the willpower method and see things as they really are.

Other emotional eaters who try to quit by the willpower method can be bad for your own desire to quit. They either talk proudly about the sacrifices they're making, or they moan about them. Either way, they reinforce the misconception that quitting demands sacrifice.

It is important that you ignore the advice of anyone who claims to have quit by the willpower method.

THE TRUTH IS THERE IS NO SACRIFICE

You are following a proven method to free you from the misery of emotional eating: A simple, logical method to unravel the brainwashing and remove all desire for junk food. It's important that you understand you are not giving anything up. Once you can see this, you win the tug-of-war. Without the tug-of-war, there is no need for willpower. Take away the fear and there is nothing to tug against. It's easy.

Nick was waiting for the moment when the struggle ended, but there is nothing to wait for. As soon as you dismantle the belief that junk food is a pleasure or comfort, you remove the desire and cure your addiction to emotional eating.

This is a thrilling moment—the moment you realize you are no longer a slave. If you've followed all the instructions and understood everything you've read so far, you should already be feeling a sense of excitement and elation.

You have taken a major step in solving your emotional eating problem and you can see where you are going.

You are in control and soon you will be free.

There is only one more potential hazard that could be holding you back from feeling like you're regaining control.

Addicts who try to quit and fail put it down to a lack of willpower. Addicts who try to quit and fail again and again put it down to something bigger, a flaw in their biological make-up, generally known as an "addictive personality."

Regardless of who you are, the only reason why anybody tries and fails to quit is because they are using the wrong method. Until you remove the desire, you will never be free from the temptation that drags you back into the trap. You have given yourself the opportunity to quit with the method that works—a method that has worked for countless addicts who have tried and failed many times with the willpower method.

So let's take any thought of personality flaws out of the equation.

Chapter 9

WHAT IF I HAVE AN ADDICTIVE PERSONALITY?

Some people believe that there is a "type" that is more prone to addiction than "normal" people, and that if you happen to be this type, there is nothing much you can do about it. The fact is, anyone can free themselves from addiction simply by following the instructions of Easyway.

Among the symptoms of emotional eating are a feeling of foolishness and weakness whenever you find yourself eating for comfort. The tug-of-war between wishing you could stop abusing your body with junk food and fearing that you couldn't cope without it creates a constant state of friction, which is confusing, frustrating, and debasing.

To overcome these disconcerting feelings, you make excuses for eating junk.

"I've been good all day, I've earned it."

"I've had a rotten week; I need a pick-me-up."

These excuses are based on the false assumption that junk food gives you pleasure or comfort, but emotional eaters need these excuses to explain away their inability to resist the urge to keep eating junk.

When you understand the nature of the trap you're in and how it controls you, it becomes clear that there is no substance to these excuses and you can't convince yourself to go along with them any more. If you've understood the point that junk food gives you nothing whatsoever—no pleasure, no comfort—then this is fine. You don't need excuses because there is no temptation.

But if you still feel the pull of temptation, despite knowing that your favorite excuses have been dismantled, you look around for another explanation. "I must have an addictive personality."

What does this mean?

In short, the addictive personality theory assumes that some people have a genetic predisposition to becoming addicted. No matter how much they try, there's something in the way they're made that turns them into addicts. It could be cigarettes, it could be heroin, it could be cake—they're bound to become hooked on something and, once they are hooked, they can't get free again. Their personality keeps them trapped.

Many addicts pounce on the addictive personality theory because it's a convenient excuse to stay in the trap. The security of the prison and the fear of success override their desire to quit and the theory gives them the excuse to stop trying. This appeals to them because:

• They believe their fix gives them pleasure or comfort.

- They perceive quitting to be hard.

- They're afraid they won't be able to cope without their little crutch.

Now ask yourself what you believe. If you go along with any of these beliefs, you need to go back and reread Chapters 6 and 7. It is essential that you understand and have no doubt whatsoever that:

- The fix gives you no pleasure or comfort whatsoever, it merely gives you temporary relief from the craving caused by the previous fix.

- Quitting is easy when there is no conflict of wills.

- Life without junk food will leave you feeling amazing compared to how you feel now.

Relying on the addictive personality theory will only insure that you remain forever trapped, your suffering increasing, and your misery leading you closer and closer to despair.

JUST ANOTHER MYTH

The addictive personality theory came about because so-called experts studying addiction noticed certain patterns among addicts that seemed to suggest a common trait. These patterns included:

- Addicts who go on craving a fix years after quitting.

- Addicts who become hooked on multiple addictions.

- Addicts who become much more seriously hooked than others.

- Addicts who share personality traits.

I've already explained why some addicts continue to feel the craving long after they've quit. Addiction is a mental condition, not a physical one, and if you quit without removing the belief that your "drug" gives you pleasure or comfort, you will always feel deprived and will always have to fight temptation.

There is a high incidence of multiple addictions—e.g. emotional eaters who are also smokers or gamblers, or heroin addicts who smoke and are heavily in debt. All these addictions are caused by the same thing, but it's not the personality of the addict: It's the misguided belief that the thing they are addicted to gives them a genuine pleasure or comfort.

THE MISERY OF THE ADDICT IS NOT RELIEVED BY THE THING THEY ARE ADDICTED TO; IT'S CAUSED BY IT

IN HER OWN WORDS: KAREN

I started smoking when I was 14. That was my first addiction. By the time I was in my 20s, I was drinking regularly too. At 22, I decided to quit smoking. I reckoned the booze was OK— all my friends were drinkers—but the smoking was becoming anti-social, not to mention costing me a fortune. To help me quit, I developed what you might call a candy habit. Instead of buying my pack of cigarettes every morning, I'd buy a couple of packs of candy. Every time I felt the craving for a smoke, I'd have a candy instead. It seemed like a sensible deal to me—a lot less money and a few more visits to the dentist instead of the threat of cancer.

But then I found myself eating more and more candy and not just that, I was craving all sorts of sweet things: Cookies, cakes, chocolate bars... I put on a lot of weight. I had always looked at obese people and thought, "Why don't you just stop eating so much before you get to that state?" But by my 23rd birthday, I was one of them, weighing in at 225 pounds, and I couldn't seem to do anything about it.

When I looked in the mirror I was disgusted by what I saw. I knew what I needed to do, but I just couldn't bring myself to do it. I was hooked on junk food. Then I heard that smoking makes you slimmer. It was the best news I'd heard for years, because I still craved cigarettes, despite my attempt to substitute them with candy, and I was desperate to lose weight. So there I was, back on the cigarettes, still on the booze, and hooked on junk food. And I tell you what, the smoking didn't make me slimmer at all. That's a complete myth.

I had turned to all these things because I'd been led to believe that they would give me pleasure, relieve my stress, make me feel better, but they were all doing the opposite. I was miserable, I was stressed and I hated myself. I was just a hopeless case, doomed to get hooked on anything addictive that came my way. It seemed obvious to me that there had to be something in the way.

I wondered what it was that made me so weak when it came to smoking, drinking, and emotional eating.

Then someone lent me *The Easy Way to Stop Smoking* and I learned from Allen Carr that addiction is not the fault of the addict; it's the fault of the society that fools us into consuming these addictive things and thinking they give us pleasure or comfort. This was a revelation. It made me see that I could quit smoking without needing candy or any other substitutes to help with the cravings because there would be no cravings. And having quit smoking, it made me see that I had the power to control my eating habits too. It just required a change of mindset, from believing that I couldn't live happily without these things to realizing that it was these things that were preventing me from living happily.

By my 25th birthday, I had quit smoking, was drinking very infrequently, and had lost 80 pounds. I can honestly say I found it easy. Once I had let go of the belief that I was doomed to be an addict, I was able to unravel the remaining illusions and the bonds that had kept me hooked weakened and dropped off.

WHY ME THEN?

So why do some people fall deeper into the trap than others? Why can one person have the occasional cookie and leave it at that, while another ends up eating the whole box?

Doesn't that suggest that one has an addictive personality and the other doesn't?

It does point to a difference between them, yes, but there are numerous differences between people that can explain why one person's behavior differs from another's in this context, and none of them has anything to do with their personality.

Our behavior is closely linked to the influences we are subjected to as we grow up: Different parents, teachers, friends, things we read, watch and listen to, places we go, people we meet, etc. These are all part of the brainwashing and they will all have a bearing on how quickly we descend into the trap. People with time and money on their hands tend to fall into the trap faster because there are no obstacles holding them back.

If you believe that junk food gives you pleasure or comfort, and each time you eat it you feel the partial relief of the craving caused by the previous fix, then your belief will increase, your desire will increase, and your determination to eat more will increase.

IT IS THE BELIEF THAT JUNK FOOD GIVES YOU PLEASURE OR COMFORT THAT HASTENS YOUR DESCENT INTO THE TRAP

BORN WEAK?

Have you ever felt you and other overeaters seem to be a different breed from everyone else? You might share similar character traits: An unstable temperament that swings between exuberance and misery, a tendency toward excess, a high susceptibility to stress, evasiveness, anxiety, insecurity. Do you feel more comfortable in the company of other overeaters?

Beware the temptation to believe that these character traits are evidence of a shared personality flaw that has doomed you all to be emotional eaters. The reality is they are the *result* of emotional eating.

All addicts feel more comfortable in the company of similar addicts, but not because they're more interesting, free-spirited, or fun. On the contrary, the attraction lies in the very fact that they won't challenge you or make you think twice about your addiction. Why? Because they're in the same boat.

All addicts know that they're doing something foolish and self-destructive. If they're surrounded by other people doing the same thing, they don't feel quite so weak.

These destructive feelings of weakness, helplessness, stupidity, and hopelessness are a terrible reality for addicts of all kinds. You will know these feelings for yourself, every time you give in to the temptation to eat junk. They are the chief cause of misery and they drive you back to your little crutch time and time again.

The good news is that once you're free from your addiction, you won't just be saved from all the unhealthy effects of overeating, you will also be liberated from the terrible impact it has on your character.

ONE FINAL STATISTICAL POINT

The addictive personality theory is based on genetics. It assumes there is a gene that predisposes some people to addiction. On that basis, there should be a fairly consistent proportion of the world's population who are addicts. Correct?

But this is not the case. Let's take smoking as our example because it's the addiction that has undergone the most research over the longest period of time. In the 1940s, over 80 percent of the U.K. adult male population were smokers; today that figure is under 20 percent. A similar trend is evident throughout most of the Western world. So are we to conclude that the proportion of people with addictive personalities has fallen by a whopping 60+ percent in just over seventy years?

While the number of smokers in the West has plummeted, the number in the East has soared. So what's happened there? Have all the people with addictive personalities migrated to Asia and vice versa?

Emotional eating and its related health risks, obesity and diabetes, are on the rise. But no one is putting this down to the addictive personality theory; they're blaming the amount of junk food on the market and the increasing brainwashing from advertisers compelling us to consume it. In the face of this barrage, you need to keep a clear head and maintain a good understanding of the trap they're trying to lure you into. Remember, when you've seen through an illusion, you cannot be fooled by it again.

It's essential that you understand that you didn't become an emotional eater because you have an addictive personality. If you think you have an addictive personality, it's simply because you got hooked on junk food.

This is the trick that addiction plays on you. It makes you feel that you're dependent on your addiction and that there's some weakness in your character or genetic make-up. It distorts your perceptions and thus maintains its grip on you.

The addictive personality theory is a serious threat to addicts because it reinforces the belief that escape is out of your hands and that you are condemned to a life of slavery and misery. This is a myth created by the illusions that junk food gives you pleasure or comfort and that quitting is hard. See through the illusions, blow away the myth and escape is easy.

The misery and slavery of emotional eating will soon be behind you as you continue to read through this book. Once you can see the situation in its true light, you'll wonder how you were ever conned into seeing it differently. Like millions of people around the world, you have been the victim of an ingenious trap. Recognize the trap for what it is, dismiss the idea of a flaw in your personality, and you will be ready to walk free.

Even if an addictive personality or gene did exist, Easyway makes it easy to break free and stay free.

Just keep an open mind and keep following all the instructions.

Chapter 10

GETTING HOOKED

We have established that your emotional eating problem is not down to a flaw in your genetic make-up, nor a weakness in your character, but to a concoction of myth and illusion that gives you a distorted perspective of your condition. You are ready now to begin your escape, unraveling the illusions one by one, starting with the reason you got hooked in the first place.

I explained in the last chapter why it is that some people become hooked on emotional eating and others don't. In Chapter 5, I explained about the void that is created from birth and makes us feel ungrounded and in need of comfort. The void is like an emptiness that needs to be filled.

We all experience the void to differing degrees because we have different experiences as we grow up. Some of us feel more driven to fill our void than others. The most common time of life to do this is in your teens, when hormones are playing havoc with your mind and body, parents are becoming a pain, pressure at school is building, and you're becoming more aware of your place in society. During this time of huge transition, disillusionment and insecurity are rife and you need something to cling to. It is the time of life when most addictions begin.

THE BRAINWASHING BEGINS

But the addiction to junk food typically starts much younger. Unlike smoking, drinking, and gambling, there is no legal age limit on eating junk food. From a very early age we learn to regard potato chips, chocolates, cakes, and other sugary confections as treats. The message is clear: "These things will make you happy." When you're given a message like that from the people you trust most, you naturally take it on board.

Parents also give their children "treats" to cheer them up when they feel sad. It's an equally clear message: "These things will comfort you."

So we grow up believing that the junk we're given as treats will give us pleasure and comfort. And who doesn't want pleasure and comfort in their life?

Of course, there are plenty of people who go through the same experience in childhood but don't develop an emotional eating problem. Are they different from you? Or are they just the flies that have yet to land on the pitcher plant? They too have been brainwashed to believe that junk food will give them pleasure or comfort; they just haven't yet felt the need to indulge. All it takes is a crisis to shake them emotionally, or, like Karen, another addiction like smoking to overcome, and they too will fall into the trap.

There are plenty of people who develop an emotional eating problem in their 30s or 40s or even later. They lived their lives with the belief that junk food could give them pleasure or comfort; the only reason they didn't get hooked sooner was because their desire had never been enough to outweigh their knowledge of the drawbacks. One trauma was enough to tip the balance.

FORBIDDEN FRUIT

It makes perfect sense that when you feel sad or insecure you should try to cheer yourself up by whatever means you believe will work. The baffling question is this: Why do we believe that we will get that pleasure or comfort from things we know to be harmful?

While our parents give us candy as treats, they also tell us that they're not good for us. We grow up fully informed about the effects of sugary foods on our teeth and our weight. Yet we also grow up seeing our parents and other responsible role models indulging in these things. So any sense that they might really do us harm is removed.

At the same time, there is something about being warned away from something that makes it all the more enticing. Don't go into the haunted house! Don't lean over the railing! Don't put your head out of the window!… What's the first thing you do when your parents aren't looking?

BY WARNING US OFF JUNK FOOD, OUR PARENTS INCREASE THE TEMPTATION TO TRY IT

This comes back to intellect overriding instinct. We've been warned against eating too many sweet things, but we've also been told they give us pleasure and comfort. Then we see our role models eating them, so we suspect their warnings must be covering something up.

"OK, so candy rots your teeth, but there must be something fantastic about it to make all these people eat it despite that danger."

"OK, so too much cake can make you obese, but it must be delicious for people to take that chance."

Rather than take the warnings at face value, our intellect looks for a hidden message: "If people are doing it in spite of all the dangers I've been warned about, there must be something great about it."

WE DEVELOP A DESIRE TO GET HOOKED

The simple truth, which we are never told, is that all those role models eat junk because they too have been brainwashed and can't get off the hook.

WHY WE CARRY ON

You first started eating junk because you were encouraged to. You were not drawn to it by a flaw in your genetic make-up or a weakness in your character. You were brainwashed into believing that it would give you pleasure or comfort.

The next question is this: If there is no genuine pleasure or comfort in eating junk, why do we continue to do it? Why, when we can see the harm it's causing us physically and feel the damage emotionally, do we not go back to the warnings and steer clear?

We cannot underestimate the power of the brainwashing. You may not be getting the pleasure or comfort you expect from eating, but that doesn't mean you've seen through the illusions. Remember the picture in Chapter 2: until you're told the three men are the same, your brain doesn't think to look at them in that way.

In the same way, the illusion that junk food gives you pleasure or comfort remains intact, even when you can't feel it. The only way to feel satisfied when you eat is to cut out the junk food, but the brainwashing is so powerful that when you don't get satisfaction from eating, you assume that you need to eat more, not less.

THE REASON YOU CONTINUE TO EAT JUNK IS THAT YOU ARE CHASING AN IMPOSSIBLE GOAL

That goal is satisfaction—the feeling of pleasure or comfort that you expect from food. Emotional eaters never feel satisfied. You only get satisfaction from eating when you quell genuine hunger with nutritious food. Satisfaction is what a healthy eater feels after every meal.

The only way you can feel satisfied is not to eat junk.

What are the feelings that typically drive you to eat junk?

- Boredom—"It's something to do and it keeps my mind occupied."

- Sadness—"It helps me forget that I'm alone."

- Stress—"It helps me to switch off and forget about my worries."

- Routine—"It's just what I do when the kids have gone to bed."

- Reward—"It's my little treat after a long, hard day."

These are not indicators of genuine pleasure. You must have had times in your life when you had a hobby that gave you genuine pleasure. Say you played tennis.

People who love tennis would play every day if they could. They wouldn't wait until they felt bored, sad, or stressed. They would break their routine for a game of tennis. And they don't feel they have to earn the right to play. They actively pursue the sport because it gives them genuine pleasure.

Next time you consider eating junk for pleasure or comfort, look more closely. Are you really doing it for pleasure or comfort, or are you doing it because something in your mind is compelling you to and making you feel uncomfortable if you don't? Examine the illusion. Can you see through it?

TWO MONSTERS

The word "addict" has always conjured up an image of the squalid drug addict. Even smokers struggle to regard themselves as addicts until they understand the nature of the trap they are in. Addict is an ugly word that no one wants as a label, so we use terms like smoker, gambler, alcoholic, and emotional eater instead.

But it is evident that all these behaviors are addictive; whether they involve a substance like nicotine, alcohol, or sugar, or a behavior like gambling or gaming, they take control of your brain in a very similar way to heroin and other hard drugs. There is a physical effect and then there is a psychological effect.

I call the physical effect the Little Monster. It is so small as to be almost imperceptible and it quickly passes, leaving a feeling of unease and emptiness like a niggling itch. The Little Monster was created the first time you ate junk. It feeds on Bad Sugar and when you don't give it what it wants, it begins to complain. This too is barely perceptible, but it is dangerous because it arouses another monster.

This second monster is not physical but psychological. I call it the Big Monster and it is created by all the brainwashing. The Big Monster interprets the Little Monster's complaints as "I need to eat junk," and so you end up trying to satisfy a craving by doing the very thing that caused the craving in the first place.

Every time you eat junk, it quietens the Little Monster, creating the illusion that the junk has made you feel better. In fact, all it has done is taken you from feeling miserable and restless to feeling slightly less so. Before you created the Little Monster you may have felt miserable and restless from time to time, but the feeling wasn't permanent. You didn't need a stimulant just to feel OK. Now you need it again and again just to feel like you're getting a bit of a lift.

But you never quite get back to where you were before you started. That's the thing with addiction. Every time you give your body a stimulant, it develops a tolerance against it.

So every time you eat junk you need to eat more to get the same boost, and every time you stop you sink lower. The longer you go on trying to satisfy the Little Monster with junk, the lower your mood sinks and the more dependent you become.

This is why emotional eating never makes you feel fulfilled.

MINDLESS EATING

Have you ever opened a box of cookies with the intention of only eating one and found yourself ten minutes later having devoured all of them? Why do we do it? There is no pleasure in it. Logic would suggest that if one cookie tastes divine, a whole box should be an Earth-moving experience, but the reality is nothing like that, is it? Physically you feel empty and sick, while emotionally you feel unsatisfied, disgusted with yourself, and horribly out of control.

The more you eat, the less you savor each cookie. It just becomes a race to stuff them all down yourself as fast as you can. Only when the box is empty can you stop. Clearly you're not eating the cookies for their flavor, you're eating them to satisfy the Little Monster.

> There is nothing to savor. The lack of satisfaction drives you to the next cookie, and the next, and the next, and the further you go without achieving satisfaction, the more frenzied and ridiculous the eating becomes. Like a dog chasing its tail, you go faster and faster chasing something you can never attain.

The low you feel as you withdraw physically (the Little Monster) is compounded by the low brought on by the psychological craving (the Big Monster) and as you slide further into the trap, the realisation of your predicament brings you down even more. This triple low becomes your new idea of normal.

Unlike the Little Monster, the Big Monster really can make you miserable. When it is awakened, it fills your head with the illusion of deprivation, reminding you of all the false ideas you've been fed about junk food being a source of pleasure and comfort, and compelling you to get another "fix."

The only "pleasure" you get is the mild relief of the withdrawal symptoms and the abandonment of control. In other words, the Little Monster is kept quiet for a while, but you know that when it awakes again its cries will be louder than ever. And the Big Monster's influence will be stronger than before. This is the cycle of addiction that keeps you in the trap, even when you know you're getting no pleasure or comfort from each fix.

FIX FIXATION

It's revealing that junkies use the word "fix." A fix is a solution to a problem; you fix something that is broken. When something breaks and you fix it, it is never quite as good as it was originally. A fix is not an improvement. It is not a pleasure or reward. It is nothing more than relief, like taking off tight shoes.

FACE YOUR FEAR

All emotional eaters wish they could feel like healthy eaters. At the same time you are afraid to "give up" your little pleasure or comfort. This conflict leaves you feeling helpless and stupid. Why can't you just take control of the situation and sort yourself out?

Unfortunately, the usual response to this confusion is for emotional eaters to bury their heads in the sand and pretend that they don't have a problem.

They lie to themselves about the state they're in and pretend that all they're doing is treating themselves to a bit of harmless indulgence. As long as you keep your head in the sand, you will not be able to see through the illusions and you will remain in the trap, suffering increasing misery every time you eat the usual junk.

The beautiful truth is that you can start feeling like a healthy eater any time you want to. All you have to do is stop eating junk. It's as easy as that, provided you understand the trap you're in and follow the right method to get out of it.

You've already taken a big step. You have overcome denial and accepted that you have an emotional eating problem. That's why you're reading this book. Now all you have to do is kill the Big Monster. Once the Big Monster is dead, you will find it easy to cut off the supply to the Little Monster and it will die very quickly and painlessly.

You kill the Big Monster by removing the illusions that create the desire to eat junk. Think about how those illusions were created and who by. The parents, friends, and other role models who all brainwashed you into believing that junk food is a pleasure or comfort were all brainwashed themselves. The advertisers who continue to peddle that message have a vested interest in you remaining hooked. Don't give them the satisfaction. You have a right to happiness and they are standing in your way.

STICK TO YOUR GUNS

Your brainwashed belief in the illusion of pleasure is what put you in the trap. Now that you understand the nature of the trap, you can see that there is no genuine pleasure in eating junk, just an illusion that drags you into a downward spiral of misery. You understand that eating junk does not fill the void; it creates it and makes it bigger. Your brain is unraveling the illusions.

YOU HAVE ALREADY BEGUN TO KILL THE BIG MONSTER

Now we need to make sure that you are not diverted from your course. There are still several things that could sabotage your escape plan. There may be a part of you that still believes you get some pleasure or comfort from eating junk.

Perhaps you are afraid that life without junk food will leave you feeling deprived. There are many influences out there that will mislead you with false ideas like these and some of them are well-meaning. Please take note of my next instruction:

FIFTH INSTRUCTION:
IGNORE ALL ADVICE AND INFLUENCES
THAT CONFLICT WITH EASYWAY

The simple truth is you are not "giving up" anything. You are freeing yourself from a trap that has been damaging your health and happiness. Rejoice! The Big Monster is dying and soon you will be ready to kill the Little Monster too.

Chapter 11

WATCH WHAT YOU EAT

The brainwashing has caused you to develop a relationship with food that isn't healthy, either physically or mentally. But you can unravel the brainwashing very quickly and restore a healthy relationship with food just by challenging the Big Monster and questioning the beliefs that have led you into the trap.

Do you ever stop to ask yourself why you eat? I don't mean why you eat the way you do. I mean why do you eat at all? The obvious answer is that you would die of starvation if you didn't eat. But is that what you're thinking whenever you eat?

We might say, "I'm starving," when we're hungry, but how many of us actually know what starvation feels like? Next time you sit down to a meal, ask yourself why you're about to eat. Isn't it more likely that the answer would be that it's what you always do at this time of day?

Ask yourself the same question next time you're buying a snack in the middle of the afternoon. You might conclude that it's habit and routine too, or perhaps you'll have been compelled by the aroma of cooking, or you just want it. You think the snack will give you pleasure.

THE FACT IS, WE DON'T PAY ATTENTION TO WHY WE'RE EATING

Routine, boredom, restlessness, stress, and anxiety are common triggers for emotional eating. They have nothing to do with avoiding starvation. We eat to fill the void and we eat to divert our attention from our problems. You have a difficult problem at work, so you reach for the cookies. They take your mind off your anxiety for a moment, but when you've finished and you return to your work, the problem is still there. A cookie doesn't take away your problems, but as long as you regard it as a comfort you will crave cookies every time you feel anxious.

People talk about the mid-afternoon "sugar low" and many use that as an excuse to reach for the cookies, or chocolate, or cake. Yet in most cases the low is caused by Bad Sugar addiction and the dysfunctional and catastrophic effect it has on blood sugar levels. Get rid of the addiction and the mid-afternoon sugar low disappears. In the event that there's a general mid-afternoon drop in energy, there are plenty of things you could turn to that will genuinely boost you and provide great nutrition, none of which are addictive.

In many cases, though, the desire to snack is generated by boredom rather than any nutritional need and that's classic emotional-eating behavior and to be avoided.

There are lots of things you can use to perk yourself up mid-afternoon; none of them should involve eating. A gossip at the water cooler, a chit-chat with a colleague, a short, mindful break. All of these generate genuine pleasures and benefits.

Why does anyone think a problem that has nothing to do with hunger can be alleviated by eating?

One reason is because that's how junk food is sold to us. Cheer yourself up with a chocolate bar. Comfort yourself with a cake. Enjoy the movie more with some salty or sugary snacks. The false belief that junk food will give pleasure or comfort (the Big Monster) makes us eat it, regardless of whether we're hungry or not.

The other reason is the cycle of addiction. Withdrawal from the previous fix adds to your anxiety. When you eat more junk, you partially relieve that withdrawal, creating the impression that the food has eased your anxiety.

REFUELING

So is the only genuine reason for eating to avoid starvation? Wouldn't that be like putting fuel in a car just to prevent it from becoming derelict? We put fuel in our cars so they will carry us around and that's exactly the same with your body. Food is the fuel your body needs to be active and energetic.

Now think about the way you refill a car. Do you follow a regular routine, putting in the same amount at the same time every day or week? Perhaps you drive a regular number of miles every week, and so you know that the gas you put in will keep your car running for the desired distance. But what if you don't use the car one week? Will you still go and put your usual amount in the tank?

We all know what would happen if you did. There would be fuel spilling out all over the gas station. Nobody refuels their car in this way, yet this is exactly how we refuel our bodies. Day after day, we follow the same routine, eating roughly the same amounts at roughly the same times, regardless of how much we've been working and how hungry we feel.

I'm not expecting you to approach every meal with a purely functional attitude, but it is important that you are under no illusion about the true, natural purpose of eating.

WE EAT FOR FUEL AND MAINTENANCE

When we don't eat for these reasons, there is no physical pleasure. The only "pleasure" is mental—the satisfaction of the Big Monster.

EATING TO EXCESS

Eating according to a fixed routine is as mindless as putting 20 gallons of fuel in your car every Tuesday and Saturday, regardless of how much driving you've done. It is the distance we have to drive that determines how much fuel we need to put in the tank, not the other way around. And if we go a week without using the car, we know not to put in any gas.

This is exactly how wild animals eat. The squirrel knows when to stop eating nuts and start storing them. Once they've eaten enough to keep themselves functioning, they stop. Humans are designed to work in the same way too, yet we've become so detached from this natural mechanism that we keep pumping in the 20 gallons of fuel even when the tank is already full.

WE LET OUR INTELLECT OVERRIDE OUR INSTINCTS

Just like the car, we can't cope with the excess. In the case of the car, the gas splashes out of the nozzle all over the gas station. But imagine if it flowed out of the tank and into the back seat and the trunk. That's effectively what happens with our bodies. The excess stays on board, stored as fat.

It only makes sense to eat a consistent amount at the same time every day if you burn off the same amount of energy every day. But that is very unlikely. One day you might work very hard and burn off a lot of energy; the next you might take a vacation, maybe spend the afternoon sitting in the backyard doing nothing at all. The fact is, when you eat healthy, nutritious food your body and brain combine automatically to insure you eat the correct amount. Overeating simply isn't an issue.

In order to avoid overfueling, all you have to do is apply the same flexible approach to eating as you do to filling your car. Wild animals don't worry about their weight or how they dispose of the food once they've digested it. All they're concerned about is finding a sufficient supply of their favorite food. Perhaps you're thinking that sounds like you. That's the whole problem, right? All you're concerned about is getting hold of your favorite food. So what's the difference?

THE EVIDENCE OF OYSTERS

The difference is that you have been brainwashed and wild animals haven't. We think we're more sophisticated than wild animals, but when it comes to choosing our favorite foods, they are much more attuned than we are.

Animals are very choosy about the food they eat. Humans, by contrast, tend to make a simple distinction between food and poison and then, based on the knowledge that poison is bad for us, assume all food is not bad for us. It's important that you understand that not all foods are suitable for your body.

If you can't trust the food manufacturers, how are you supposed to know which foods are good for you and which are not? Well, wild animals manage it and they're much less intelligent than you.

The senses of sight, touch, smell, and taste are all an animal needs to find its favorite food and make sure it doesn't eat anything that's bad for it.

An animal will approach its food with caution. It will look, it will sniff, it will prod, and it will lick, all before taking a mouthful of food. With each sense, it is testing the food before swallowing any of it.

It's an ingenious system and it works like a dream, so why doesn't it work for us? If Mother Nature created all this for wild animals, why did she make so many things that are bad for us, like cream cakes, chocolate bars, fries and potato chips, seem so appealing to our senses? Why didn't she apply the same logic to human beings and make the things that are bad for us taste bad and the things that are good for us taste good?

It may surprise you to learn that that's exactly what she did.

The senses are so sophisticated and the way they work together so intricate that animals are able to detect when something is bad for them without any need for intellect. All they have to do is trust their senses.

We rely on labels with sell-by dates to tell us when food is going off. Wild animals don't need sell-by dates because the rotting process sends its own signals to the senses. As a natural food begins to putrify, it changes in look, smell and feel, repulsing the senses that were previously attracted to it.

Think about an apple. That shiny, taut skin turns brown and speckled with mold; the sweet, delicate smell turns acrid and strong; the crisp flesh becomes soft and mushy. It will taste foul too, but you don't need to get that far. Your other senses will have warned you off.

The detection system doesn't stop there. If you do happen to consume something poisonous, the warning lights will come on. You'll feel sick. You will probably get diarrhea. Your digestive system will do everything it can to eject the poison. You may get a headache and fever. We habitually see these warning signs as a problem in themselves and treat them with a painkiller or some other medicine to bring our temperature down, but the fever is the body's self-defense mechanism kicking into action. If you're constantly taking indigestion remedies, you're ignoring the warning that you're poisoning your body.

Remember, your choice of food is heavily influenced by brainwashing. Your intellect has been bombarded with false messages about the pleasure and comfort you can get from junk food and you've been conditioned to trust your intellect over your instincts.

How do you feel about oysters? There's a food that divides opinion. A lot of people detest the very idea of oysters. They've never tasted one to confirm their aversion; they just know by looking that they're not going to like them. Others do try them, but find the feel, smell, and taste revolting. Once upon a time, oysters were low-cost fodder for poor people who couldn't afford better, yet now they're sold as a delicacy. But ask anyone who loves oysters what they felt the first time they ate them, and most will admit to finding them as revolting as they look. They had to work hard to overcome their instincts before they could convince themselves they were a pleasure.

Why would anyone put themself through that? Because intellectually they've been led to believe that there will be a reward if they can get beyond the initial revulsion.

Smokers and drinkers go through the same initial revulsion. They have to force themselves to smoke or drink again until their senses become immune. This is how we force our instincts to give way to our intellect. Strip away the brainwashing and the truth stands out bright and clear:

THE FOODS THAT TASTE BEST FOR YOU ARE THE BEST FOR YOU

MAKE AN INFORMED CHOICE

We've been given all the tools we need to make sure we get hold of our favorite foods, yet we seldom use them. In short, we don't pay attention to the food we eat. We don't ask ourselves why we're eating and we don't ask ourselves whether we're really enjoying the food. We eat like mindless drivers, filling our tanks regardless of whether it's the right fuel or there's room in the tank.

Remember, there are a lot of people with a vested interest in keeping you hooked on junk food and they really don't care about the emotional damage it does. But you can easily escape from the trap by paying attention to the food you eat and asking yourself what it's really doing for you. Your senses haven't died; they've just been sidelined. You'll be amazed how quickly they leap back into action when you give them some attention.

And when you listen to your senses, you'll begin to unravel the brainwashing very quickly too. Up until now you haven't really been exercising your own choice over the food you eat because you've been brainwashed into choosing what the junk food peddlers want you to choose. By bringing your senses back into play, you'll be able to make a genuinely informed choice about what your favorite foods are—a choice informed by your own personal detection system.

Paying attention to your senses helps to insure you put the right kind of fuel in your tank. In the next chapter we'll look at the natural fuel gauge that tells you when to fill up and when to stop filling.

Chapter 12

HUNGER

IN THIS CHAPTER

• *THE CONNECTION BETWEEN HUNGER AND TASTE*
• *READING YOUR NATURAL FUEL GAUGE* • *KNOWING WHEN TO STOP*
• *REAL v. FALSE HUNGER* • *THIS IS NOT A DIET*

Our built-in detection system doesn't just tell us what to eat but also when. Just as the car manufacturer came up with the fuel gauge, Mother Nature gave us our own fuel gauge. Hunger is what tells wild animals when they need to feed. And hunger is our one true reason for eating.

Not only has Mother Nature given us a sensation that tells us when we need to eat, but one that also compels us to get up and do something about it. We humans have a tendency to exaggerate. "I'm starving" or "I'm famished" are common ways of saying "I feel hungry." If you have ever experienced starvation, I doubt you would use the word so lightly. Starvation is agony. What we call hunger is anything but. In fact, hunger is a sensation that contributes to the enjoyment of eating.

Satisfying your hunger is one of the greatest pleasures in life and, provided that you follow your natural guide and all of my instructions, it's one that you can enjoy more than once a day, every day, for the rest of your life.

THE CONNECTION BETWEEN HUNGER AND TASTE

What if you can't satisfy your hunger as soon as you feel it? How much of a pain does it become? Your stomach might rumble, but that's hardly painful, is it? Any suffering you experience is purely psychological. If you tell yourself you're being deprived, you'll feel annoyed and you'll regard hunger as a source of misery.

This is why diets are so grueling and ultimately unsuccessful. Because you begin with a sense of deprivation, every time you feel hungry that sense deepens and the more miserable you feel. That's hardly the right mindset for making a positive change.

You can turn this feeling around simply by telling yourself to see hunger in a different light: not as a threat that needs to be dealt with right away but as a source of pleasure that will increase the longer you leave it.

The French say "bon appetit" before they eat. The French are renowned food lovers and they devote a lot of time to the pleasure of eating. They understand that the greater your appetite, the more you'll enjoy the meal. They recognize that there is a direct association between hunger and taste.

You need to be hungry to get the full pleasure from the taste of food. Indeed, the more hungry you get, the more ready your taste buds are to enjoy a range of foods.

Are you ready for your next instruction?

SIXTH INSTRUCTION:
AVOID EATING UNLESS YOU ARE HUNGRY

The real pleasure in eating is derived from satisfying your hunger. You may be thinking this is at odds with what I said at the beginning of Chapter 2, that eating should be a pleasure and that we've been designed to enjoy our food. If the pleasure we derive from eating is merely the satisfying of hunger, is that not the same as wearing tight shoes just to feel the relief of taking them off?

Let me remind you at this point that the fundamental purpose of this book is to help you get the maximum pleasure from life by solving your eating problem. It is not to inflict more misery on you. Hunger is not miserable unless you are in the desperate situation of having no food and being unable to satisfy your hunger. But I'm not talking about starvation, I'm talking about hunger—the natural signal that lets you know when your tank is running low.

Wearing tight shoes is very uncomfortable; hunger is not. Yet satisfying hunger is every bit as pleasurable as taking off tight shoes. Such is the ingenuity of our in-built detection mechanism. Provided we follow our instincts, we get all the pleasure and none of the pain.

Pleasure and enjoyment are part of our natural mechanism for survival. In other words, pleasure is not just a bonus that we create for ourselves when we can find the time or the money; it is fundamental to our existence!

We all know how rewards work. When a child does something good, its parent rewards it with a hug or a treat to encourage the child to repeat the good behavior. When we eat the right foods, nature rewards us with a feeling of pleasure to encourage us to continue to seek out those foods.

If you find that you are not enjoying life, it is because you have been led astray from this natural reward system and brainwashed with false rewards. By paying attention to your senses and your natural fuel gauge, you can reconnect with your natural reward system and make a clear distinction between the genuine and false pleasures of eating.

READING YOUR NATURAL FUEL GAUGE

Hunger is the natural signal that it is time to refuel. The longer you go hungry, the better the food will taste and the more pleasure you will get from eating. Obviously you don't want to starve yourself, so when is the optimum time to satisfy your hunger?

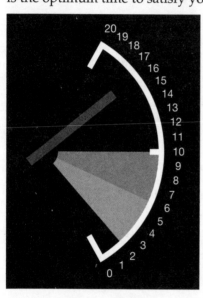

To help answer this question, think of hunger as a fuel gauge numbered from 0 to 20, where 0 is empty and 20 is full up.

On this gauge, 10 is the point at which hunger is satisfied, the range between 7 and 10 is slight hunger, and the range between 3 and 7 is true hunger.

When the needle drops to true hunger, that is when you should be looking to eat. You may feel the first hint of hunger as the needle hovers between 7 and 10, but don't take this as a sign to eat at once, or you will not get the full pleasure from the food. The true hunger you feel between 3 and 7 is not painful or threatening. In fact, if your mind is occupied with other things you probably won't even notice it.

Slight hunger can be made to feel like true hunger by factors such as the smell of food or the sight of it. If you feel slight hunger and somebody starts talking to you about the lovely meal they ate in a restaurant the previous evening, it will make you feel more hungry than you really are. Food advertisers use this as one of their chief weapons. They know that if they can put their food in front of you in some shape or form, you will think you are hungry and will feel more inclined to want it.

The key is to pay attention to your hunger. Feel it. Enjoy it. Remember, hunger is the signal that pleasure is on its way.

When you start paying attention to your hunger, it doesn't take long to develop a good understanding of where your needle is on the gauge at any given time. This will go a long way to helping you solve your emotional eating problem. Up until now the junk food peddlers have had a field day making you think you need to eat when you don't; now you can turn the tables and feel for yourself when you need to eat and when you don't.

Hunger is a natural signal to find food and it becomes more and more of an impulse as it grows but, like the fuel gauge in a car, it gives you plenty of notice. As a result of the brainwashing, however, we've come to regard hunger as a signal to eat NOW! Most of us rarely feel slight hunger, let alone true hunger, because we eat according to routine or emotional need. When we do feel hunger, we interpret it as the tank being empty and we panic a little. "Wow! I'm hungry. I need to eat something now." We assume it's going to become painful.

Believe me, you have a long way to go before it becomes painful.

You have no reason to fear hunger and no reason to panic. You can eat any time you want and nobody is telling you to deprive yourself. Unlike wild animals, you don't have to risk your life going out to get it. All you have to do is follow your natural fuel gauge and everything you eat will be a pleasure.

KNOWING WHEN TO STOP

When you eat according to true hunger, everything you eat tastes better. This is a wonderful feeling, so much so that it can be distracting.

It can take your mind off your fuel gauge but shouldn't lead you to you overeating.

The fuel gauge doesn't just tell you when to eat; it tells you when to stop too.

We've established that the range from 3 to 7 on the gauge is true hunger—this is the best time to eat. Between 7 and 10 is slight hunger —the time when hunger is often imperceptible and eating now will not give the same amount of pleasure. At 10, hunger is satisfied—this is the time to stop eating.

If you keep eating beyond 10 on the gauge, the food will give you no pleasure and you will start to feel uncomfortable. Continue to eat until the gauge reaches 20 and you will be left feeling completely full up and bloated. When you eat healthy, nutritious food, it's extremely unlikely to happen.

> ### EAT SLOWLY TO AVOID OVEREATING
>
> As you learn to pay attention to your hunger gauge, be aware that there is a time lag between eating and this registering on your fuel gauge. Eat too fast and you run the risk of overeating before your fuel gauge has registered that you are satisfied. Make a point of eating slowly to give your body time to register that it has received the nutrients it requires. The French like to make a meal last for hours: It gives them time to savor each mouthful and to chat between mouthfuls. This has been proven to be a very healthy way of eating.

Eating beyond the point of satisfaction is what gives you that bloated, uncomfortable feeling that can leave a bad taste in the mouth—literally.

But if our natural fuel gauge is so sophisticated, why do we ever feel the desire to continue eating beyond the point of satisfaction? Surely it should send a strong signal to stop before we go too far.

In fact, that's exactly what it does. The problem is that we've been conditioned to ignore it. We are so brainwashed by the constant bombardment of mixed messages about what we should be eating, we've lost touch with our own natural gauge. As you reconnect with your own hunger and learn to gauge it for yourself, you will start to recognize the signals that tell you when to stop eating as well as when to start. Avoiding Bad Sugar will also insure that you no longer overeat. It's the nutritionally invalid foods, containing refined sugar, and processed, starchy carbs, that promote overeating.

Your natural fuel gauge is designed to register "satisfied" once you've taken in sufficient nutrients. The signal it gives you is the removal of all desire to carry on fueling. You can demonstrate this for yourself right now by drinking a glass of water. I guarantee you will want to stop drinking as soon as your thirst is quenched, not when your belly is full.

Water is the most essential fuel for human survival and we can feel very clearly when we need to drink and when we need to stop drinking. Corrupt that water with junk, however, such as alcohol or sugar, and you will lose connection with your gauge. This is why people are able to drink large volumes of alcoholic drinks on a night out—because their desire to drink is not coming from their fuel gauge; it's coming from their addiction to sugar or alcohol. As far as the fuel gauge is concerned, they are not topping up on nutrients.

If the food you eat does not contain the nutrients your body requires, it will not register on the gauge and the only thing that will stop you eating is when you are full and can physically take no more. There are lots of people who say they could happily eat potato chips for hours. This is because chips never leave you feeling satisfied. As far as your fuel gauge is concerned, there's always room for more because the nutritional value of potato chips is virtually zero.

When you regularly eat foods that do not contain the required nutrients, overeating becomes the norm. It is important that you remember this fact:

LACK OF NUTRIENTS LEADS TO OVEREATING

Only by eating the right foods will you achieve a feeling of satisfaction. And only by achieving satisfaction will you know when to stop eating. But first you have to reverse the brainwashing that has prevented you from recognizing your favorite foods and realizing when you have eaten enough.

The principle for knowing when to eat and when to stop eating is very simple: Eat when you're hungry and stop when you're satisfied. Stick to this principle and you will find that every meal becomes enjoyable and you will stop associating food with emotional needs.

REAL V. FALSE HUNGER

As you become more attuned to your hunger, be aware that junk food addiction causes a false hunger that can confuse you into thinking it's time to fill the tank. The Little Monster—the physical craving for your fix of junk food—is a very slight, empty sensation that feels like genuine hunger.

As you know, the Little Monster starts crying for more as your body experiences withdrawal from the last fix of junk food. The more junk you eat, the more the feeling intensifies. For some emotional eaters, this means living with an almost constant craving, which leaves them with two choices: Fight the temptation and feel miserable, or keep grazing on junk... and feel miserable.

The only way to get rid of this false hunger is to stop eating junk food. Until you reach that point, there are some questions you can ask yourself to help distinguish between real and false hunger.

How quickly has it come on?
False hunger comes on quite suddenly, whereas real hunger grows over time.

What am I craving?
Real hunger is a craving for food in general, whereas false hunger tends to make you fixate on specific foods—sugary, salty, or fatty junk foods.

How hungry am I?
Is the compulsion to eat in proportion with the physical feeling of hunger? False hunger can make you start panicking for food when your hunger gauge is well above the true hunger zone (between 3 and 7 on your hunger gauge). If your mind is telling you to eat but your body is feeling only a slight craving, that'll be the two monsters grumbling.

THIS IS NOT A DIET

One final point about the sixth instruction: It's important that you don't regard it as an instruction to diet. I am not asking you to deprive yourself. When you pay attention to your senses and your natural fuel gauge, you can eat as much of your favorite foods as you want to. The key words are "as you want to." The desire for food is ultimately what makes you eat. True desire comes from true hunger and stops when you're satisfied.

Is it really a restriction to stop eating when you're satisfied? Why would you want to go on eating beyond that point? Do you like the idea of feeling bloated and guilty? The sixth instruction will help you rediscover the beautiful truth provided by Mother Nature:

EATING IS A PLEASURE; OVEREATING IS A PAIN

Chapter 13

YOUR FAVORITE FOOD

IN THIS CHAPTER
• WHAT HAPPENS WHEN YOU EAT JUNK • THE INCREDIBLE MACHINE
• TUNE IN TO TASTE • THE SPICE OF LIFE • THE JUNK MARGIN

If you've been brainwashed into having a preference for foods that offer no nutritional benefit, does this mean that the foods you think are your favorites are just an illusion too? And if it does, are there even more enjoyable foods that have been kept hidden from you by the brainwashing?

In Chapter 7, we examined the two fears that keep you in the trap: The fear of failure, which discourages addicts from attempting to quit, and the fear of success, which convinces them that they don't even want to.

For emotional eaters, the fear of success is based on the false belief that life without your addiction to foods that you know are doing you no good will be miserable—yes, even more miserable than life with them. This assumes that these foods give you pleasure or comfort. They don't, but I don't expect you to just take my word for it. Let's examine the evidence.

You probably have a good idea about the health risks of eating too much junk food: Heart disease, high blood pressure, Type 2 diabetes, chronic obesity and cancer, not to mention the more obvious heartburn, constipation, diarrhea, stiff joints, tooth decay, and poor skin. Do you believe nature would have designed humans—and only humans—to have a preference for foods that threaten our existence?

The knowledge of these health risks creates another fear, which is the fear that compels addicts to be permanently unhappy about their addiction. The tug-of-war between this fear and the two aforementioned fears keeps you in a constant state of turmoil, confusion, and insecurity.

Sadly, the fear of the health risks is not enough on its own to compel emotional eaters to stop. If it were, I would happily use it to scare you into quitting. But I know from experience with all addictions that scare tactics don't work. The fear of success is always pulling you back.

Instead, we need to unravel the illusion that junk food gives you pleasure or comfort.

THE INCREDIBLE MACHINE

The human body is a truly incredible machine that can withstand an enormous amount of abuse and continue to function. But don't be misled into thinking this means you can consume anything you like without doing yourself any damage. Eating the wrong type of food may not stop you in your tracks as diesel will stop a petrol car, but it does slow you down. When you don't eat the food that nature has designed for you, you become heavy, slow, lethargic… and eventually you will grind to a halt.

Deep down, you know this is true, yet the brainwashing has replaced instinctive truth with enticing illusions.

This doesn't happen when it comes to refueling a car. You don't need to understand a single thing about the workings of an engine to be aware that you shouldn't put diesel in a petrol engine and vice versa.

The majority of drivers never dream of trying to fix or service their car's engine, yet they know that it won't do it any good if they put pancake syrup where the oil should go. It's a simple, basic understanding, handed out by the experts who made the car, and we take it as read.

The animal kingdom has evolved to be every bit as sophisticated as the automobile industry. Every creature on the planet has developed its own specific diet, and with it the physical attributes to handle that diet. Only the right foods will achieve satisfaction. Hunger and taste are two of those attributes.

Digestion is another. The human digestive system works best when digesting fruit, vegetables, nuts, and seeds. It works quickly and efficiently, extracts large volumes of nutrients and leaves little waste. Digesting these foods requires relatively little energy, compared to digesting meat, for example. Ever wondered why carnivores sleep so much? A diet of fruit, vegetables, nuts, and seeds will leave you feeling more awake and energetic than a diet of hamburgers, chocolate, and cake.

So why aren't fruit, vegetables, nuts, and seeds our favorite foods? Why don't we curl up in front of the TV with a bowl of carrots? Why don't we comfort ourselves with an apple? The very thought is enough to frighten off junk food addicts from trying to quit.

Perhaps you fear a life of carrots and apples, deprived of fast food and cake and all those "delicious" treats you turn to for comfort. The fear of success is based on the belief that you'll be left with a miserable diet. But if carrots and apples are among the foods we're designed to eat, why would they make you miserable?

We've become so hoodwinked into believing junk food is the most delicious thing on the menu that we don't even consider fruit and vegetables as pleasure food; we see them as health food.

But ask yourself a question. After eating fruit or vegetables (perhaps salad), have you ever felt:

- Bloated?

- Sick?

- Guilty?

- Ashamed?

- Sad?

- Out of control?

Isn't it time you started seeing that health food and pleasure food are the same thing? Our incredible machine is designed to enjoy consuming healthy foods like fruit, vegetables, nuts, and seeds. The trouble arises when we stop believing it.

TUNE IN TO TASTE

"But I don't think about digestion when I eat; I think about the taste." Fair point. Our favorite foods are the ones that taste best, not the ones that we can digest most easily. So what tastes best? Flour? Salt? Cooking fat? Milk? These are the fundamental ingredients of cakes and cookies that many people say they couldn't live without. Of the four, only salt has more than a very mild effect on the tastebuds, and who likes the taste of salt on its own? It is only the addition of refined sugar that makes us think these foods are tasty, because refined sugar replicates the taste of the natural sugars found in fruit and vegetables and fools our sense of taste into registering that we're getting our favorite food.

It's these sugars that trigger the sense of reward. Refined sugar delivers a bigger than natural hit to the brain, and so like a drug it hijacks the reward pathways. It has other harmful effects too. Refined sugar passes into the bloodstream very quickly and causes a spike that corrupts your body's glucose and insulin balance, leading to Type 2 diabetes.

The sugar in fruit and vegetables takes longer to break down, and so passes into the bloodstream more slowly, causing a much more moderate spike, delivering a manageable supply of hormone to the reward pathways, and enabling insulin levels to adjust more gently.

As the effects of a refined sugar hit wear off, you are left feeling empty and craving another fix. You will recognize this: It's the cycle of addiction.

IT'S NOT TASTE THAT MAKES YOU EAT CAKES AND BISCUITS; IT'S SUGAR

Next time you eat a cake or a cookie, pay attention to the taste. Try not to scoff it down as quickly as you can, hold it in your hand and examine its appearance and smell. When you take a bite, keep it in your mouth for a while and examine the effect on your taste buds. Compare what you're feeling with your own senses to the expectations you've acquired through brainwashing. Does the food live up to your expectations? Is it really delicious?

As you make a habit of paying attention to your food in this way, you will start to roll back the layer of mystique and see all junk food for what it really is—relatively tasteless, odourless, and mostly brown in colour.

Now compare that with an apple. A fresh apple looks enticing. The skin is taut and shiny, with an appealing green or red color. It has a fresh, fruity aroma, and when you bite into it the aroma is matched by the taste: It's fresh, juicy, and satisfying.

An apple doesn't leave you feeling bloated or sick, guilty or ashamed. Perhaps it would if you ate enough apples all at once. But the point is you don't, because when you finish an apple, you don't immediately feel like eating another one. Your fuel gauge detects the high nutrient content and registers "satisfied."

Your perception of taste is essential to your escape from the emotional eating trap. Once you can open your mind and accept that your favorite foods are the ones that really do taste best, not the ones you think taste best, your desire for junk food will disappear and you'll find it easy to escape the cycle of addiction.

YOU WON'T NEED ANY WILLPOWER TO RESIST THE TEMPTATION TO EAT JUNK BECAUSE THERE WILL BE NO TEMPTATION

THE SPICE OF LIFE

Perhaps the thought of eating an apple whenever you feel hungry seems depressingly limited. Of course, I'm not advising you to live the rest of your life on a diet of apples. There are so many other favorite foods to choose from.

And this brings us to one of the greatest myths surrounding the food available to us: The myth that by cutting out junk food you will lose all the variety and interest in your diet.

Walk around a supermarket and you can't help being dazzled by the incredible array of different food products on sale. Yet how much of that huge variety do you incorporate in your regular diet?

Next time you go to the supermarket, count the number of different foods in your basket. It's a tiny proportion of all the products available. Now think how often you change the items on your shopping list. There may be the odd change from week to week, depending on the weather, or your mood, or your budget, but the majority of items will be the same week in week out.

ADDICTS ARE NOT INTERESTED IN VARIETY

Despite the thousands of options available to them, smokers go out of their way to obtain their usual brand. But it's not just smokers; we all tend to do the same with food. There are millions of different foods to choose from and yet we stick to the same handful of options, week after week, month after month, year after year.

YOUR USUAL, SIR?

There may be a great variety of foods available to us, but our need for such variety is an illusion. I can offer two examples from my own experience that illustrate this quite clearly. Like many people, I used to begin the day with a bowl of cereal. My local supermarket had a whole aisle devoted to the different brands of breakfast cereal, but when I sat down to eat each morning I would reach for the same every day.

It didn't bother me that I wasn't sampling all the different cereals on offer. I would happily eat the same one every day for months, even years on end. If I did ever get the urge for a change, I would pick a new cereal and that would become my regular for a similar length of time.

Then I realized one day that the ingredients of all these cereals were virtually the same anyway, even in those packages of different cereals that they call a "variety pack."

The second example of this struck me one evening when I was out for a curry. There were a lot of Indian restaurants near my house, but I had my favorite—the Motspur Park Tandoori. As I sat there perusing the menu, the owner, Malik, came over to take my order. Before I could say anything, he started announcing dishes as if he was reading them off a list. He knew exactly what I wanted.

How? Because I ordered the same thing every time!

It wasn't just at the Tandoori either—it was the same story when I went out for any sort of meal. I hadn't even realized it myself. I would sit poring over the mouthwatering descriptions on the menu, trying to make a decision. And every time I would choose the same dishes that I knew I loved.

The message is clear:

ONCE WE HAVE DECIDED ON A FAVORITE FOOD, WE ARE HAPPY TO EAT IT TIME AFTER TIME

We only think variety is important because we've been brainwashed to think that. We have been told that we need a balanced diet for the body's nutritional requirements and also that a varied diet is more interesting. But how much do you really want variety? When you go out for a meal and spend ages looking through the menu, aren't you just looking for the dish that you know you like?

There is nothing wrong with that as long as that meal provides the energy and nutrients that your body requires.

If variety really is important to you, let's pay another visit to the supermarket. The aisle where you will find the greatest variety of foods in terms of appearance, aroma, texture, shape, and taste, is what?

The fruit and vegetable aisle.

Unlike the cereals, cakes, or cookies section, every item in the fruit and vegetable aisle has its own distinctive taste. Apples, oranges, bananas, pineapples, raspberries... you could never confuse their flavors. Even fruits that are closely related, such as oranges and lemons, raspberries and strawberries, taste distinct from one another.

IF IT'S VARIETY YOU WANT IN A SUPERMARKET, LOOK NO FURTHER THAN FRUIT AND VEGETABLES

It's no coincidence that most supermarkets place their fruit and vegetables in the primary position where you start your shopping trip. Immediately your senses are thinking "delicious food!"

Consider this and remove any preconceptions that following my method will restrict the choice of foods available to you and that you will be left feeling deprived.

The opposite is true. You will be able to look forward to eating even more than you do now, but the enjoyment you feel will be genuine, not something that you have been brainwashed into believing is a pleasure.

You'll know the difference because you'll feel a sense of satisfaction after eating, instead of the sense of discomfort, guilt, and shame that comes with emotional eating. You will feel healthy and energetic too, rather than overweight and sluggish.

Once you have identified your favorite food, you'll be happy to eat it time after time.

THE JUNK MARGIN

The gorilla's favorite food is fruit, but when fruit is not available it will eat other vegetation to survive. When fruit is available again, the gorilla will revert to a fruit diet because fruit is its favorite food—the food that tastes best to the gorilla.

Does the gorilla know that if it doesn't eat anything it will die, and so make a conscious decision to force down some other vegetation when fruit is unavailable? Or does it move on to other vegetation by instinct? It doesn't taste as good as fruit, so why else would it eat it? Remember the association between hunger and taste: As the gorilla grows hungrier, so its secondary food options taste better and better.

Mother Nature has built this fail-safe in to her design to insure that animals can survive when their favorite foods are unavailable. The gorilla doesn't have to make any conscious decision. Its hunger and taste buds make the decision for it. The secondary food options have no ill effects: They don't make the gorilla overweight or suffer gastric problems. Nor does the gorilla get brainwashed into thinking that these are now its favorite foods.

This is good news for the gorilla. It's also good news for us because while Mother Nature has provided us with a specific selection of favorite foods, she has also allowed a liberal margin for error. As long as we consume mainly the foods that were designed for us, we can go on eating a fair amount of secondary foods.

Please note, this is NOT a "junk food margin"; it just means that we can allow secondary foods into our diet without fear of them causing a problem.

If fresh fruit, vegetables, nuts, and seeds are our natural favorite foods, then we could describe meat, fish, and pulses as secondary foods. They should ideally be avoided or at least kept to a minimum on our plate. Make fresh vegetables and salads the main feature of a meal with, if you want, a small portion of secondary food.

In Chapter 1, I explained that I would be using the term "junk food" to describe any processed food that lacks the nutritional content the human body requires. To most people it means fast food, cakes, and confectionery—the sort of food that nutritionists all tend to agree are bad for us. My idea of junk food is anything that is not in its natural state, anything that has been tampered with.

As you can imagine, this includes a vast number of foods that you've probably always considered healthy, such as milk and cheese. Don't worry, I'm not trying to frighten you out of consuming milk and cheese. I just want you to be clear what type of foods fall into the package that nature intended for us and what fall into the Junk Margin.

Where the Junk Margin has become a problem for the human race is in giving people the opportunity to spread misinformation about certain foods for personal gain. Imagine you were in the food business and the only foods anybody ate were those in their natural state. It wouldn't be a very big market, would it? There wouldn't be many opportunities to expand it and make good money.

Thanks to the Junk Margin, the food industry is able to package a vast array of different foods and sell them to us, often at high prices. How do they do this? By convincing us that these foods are what we most want to eat. They'll try anything, from making out that a chocolate bar is somehow good for your child, to admitting that a cake is bad for you, so it must be delicious to make you want it so much. And you do want it, don't you? Why? Because you're constantly being told that you do.

Human intellect and the ability it gives people to spread misinformation have made Junk Margin foods your first choice and the primary foods that you're designed to eat have become secondary choices. Once you recognize this, you can use your intellect to reverse the brainwashing process.

Apply your powers of image-building to the correct foods rather than junk foods. Pay attention to the real taste of everything you eat, the way it looks, smells, and feels before you eat it and the way it makes you feel afterward. Remind yourself of the health benefits of fruit, vegetables, nuts, and seeds, and the health risks of eating junk food. Acknowledge the wide variety of tastes and textures in the fruit and vegetable aisle, and the dreary similarity of all the options in the cereal aisle, or the cookie aisle, pasta, baking products, and so on.

By opening your mind to these realities, you will be able to establish control over your use of the Junk Margin, so you don't ever feel restricted to a diet of fruit and vegetables, but you never feel like a slave to junk again either.

This is true control over your eating. The difference is that your perception of the foods available to you has become true and real, not an illusion.

SEVENTH INSTRUCTION:
NEVER AGAIN EAT FOOD FOR COMFORT

Chapter 14

LINGERING QUESTIONS

IN THIS CHAPTER

• HOW WILL I KNOW WHEN I'M CURED?
• REPLACE UNCERTAINTY WITH KNOWLEDGE • WILL I BE ABLE TO ENJOY
THE GOOD TIMES? • WILL I BE ABLE TO ENDURE THE BAD TIMES?
• THE MOMENT OF REVELATION

When you achieve something big, there is a moment when you know you've made it—a moment of revelation. But when your achievement is to stop doing something that's been troubling you, how can you be sure you've stopped for good? Let's address this and some of the other uncertainties that you might be feeling right now.

Everything you've read so far has been aimed at changing your mindset: From believing that junk food gives you the pleasure or comfort you need to understanding that it actually creates and adds to the need.

You should be absolutely clear now that your emotional eating problem is not due to any weakness in your character, be it a lack of willpower or an addictive personality, nor to anything special about the food you eat.

You should also be starting to re-assess your choice of favorite foods by paying attention to your senses and hunger.

If you have any lingering doubts about any of these aspects, please go back and read the relevant chapters now. Remember to keep an open mind and listen to your instincts, not the Big Monster in your brain.

It's essential that you achieve the right mindset to enable you to walk free from the trap without a painful struggle or any feeling of deprivation. You will know when you have achieved that because you will realize that the desire that keeps driving you back to eat junk has gone.

When you started reading this book, you were probably eager to know how long it would take to work. How long would you have to wait before you could call yourself cured?

When you quit with the willpower method, you can never be sure that you've succeeded. It is a lifelong struggle to resist temptation. With Easyway, you know when you've succeeded because you remove the temptation altogether.

REPLACE UNCERTAINTY WITH KNOWLEDGE

Different people reach this stage of the book in different frames of mind. Some are confident that they understand everything and feel certain they are ready to quit. If that's you, I am delighted, but let's not jump the gun. You may be convinced that you never want to eat another cake or chocolate bar and that you will never try to comfort yourself with food again, but beware! The trap has ways of catching you out just when you least expect it.

It's important that you complete the book, so that you can walk free with all the protection you need to make sure you never fall into the trap again.

If, on the other hand, you have reached this stage in the book still uncertain that you have what it takes to overcome your emotional eating, don't worry. We still have some ground to cover and all will become clear. Whatever your current frame of mind, take the time and care to read right to the end of the book.

We need to make sure that you completely let go of any lingering belief in the willpower method. In Chapter 8, I explained how the reliance on willpower actually makes it harder to quit and more likely that you will fall back into the trap. Yet the brainwashing is so incessant that it can take a while to shake off the belief that overcoming the desire to eat junk will be incredibly hard.

There is nothing stupid or unusual in that belief. The desperate yearning you get when you try to deny your desire for junk food may go against all logic, but the feeling is still very real and so is the irritability and misery you feel when you try to use willpower to stop. You've been subjected to the brainwashing all your life and if you've ever tried to quit by using the willpower method, you will have reinforced the belief that it's hard.

ANY FAILED ATTEMPT TO CONTROL YOUR EATING THROUGH WILLPOWER REINFORCES THE BELIEF THAT IT IS DIFFICULT TO STOP

When you're convinced that willpower is the solution, you blame yourself for your failures. This adds to your misery and low self-esteem and drives you deeper into the trap.

Free yourself from any belief in the willpower method and all of a sudden this vicious circle goes into reverse. Stop pushing against the wrong side of the door, open your mind to there being an easy way out, and that easy way will open up to you as if by magic. Of course, it's not magic, it's simple logic—a logic we're all blinded to by the brainwashing.

But when you open your mind and let the truth in, it can feel miraculous—a moment of revelation.

The truth is very simple:

- The desire comes from the Big Monster—the illusion that eating junk gives you pleasure or comfort.

- The anxiety you feel when you can't eat junk is merely the Big Monster responding to the cries of the Little Monster to be fed.

- The Little Monster was created by eating junk in the first place.

- Therefore, eating junk does not relieve the anxiety; it causes it.

Kill the Big Monster and you remove any feeling of deprivation when you stop eating junk.

The willpower method is all about fighting through the anxiety for long enough until you no longer feel it. In the first few days after quitting when your willpower is at its strongest, you will have the upper hand in the battle.

But over time, as you begin to believe you're winning, your willpower will inevitably slacken off.

They say a football team is most vulnerable just after scoring. It's the same with the willpower method. It's when you think you're winning that you're at your most vulnerable. You can't maintain the effort it took to quit and your motivation to do so lessens. Then one day you notice the Little Monster crying to be fed and the Big Monster awakens with a roar. It's very hard to dig in again and you feel victory slipping from your grasp.

Now your mind is torn in two, one half determined to stay off the junk, the other urging you to tuck in. Is it surprising that we get so confused, irritable, and downright miserable on the willpower method? It would be a miracle if we didn't!

If you're worried that you might fall back into the trap at some point after you've quit because that's what you've done before, remember that it is the Big Monster that pulls you back in. You have all the ammunition you need to kill the Big Monster. Pay attention to your senses and hunger, clear your mind of the illusions, see the true picture, and you will walk free with absolute certainty that you have no desire to seek pleasure or comfort in junk food again.

WILL I BE ABLE TO ENJOY THE GOOD TIMES?

This is a very important question. What's the point in life without pleasure? This book is all about helping you put the pleasure back into your life. The problem has been that you've been trying to do that by eating junk food. You should now be clear that the solution is to NOT eat junk food.

But if you've spent years of your life believing that junk food gives you pleasure or comfort, you might be concerned that living the rest of your life without any junk food at all will be a bit miserable.

The truth is that addiction to junk food actually reduces your ability to derive pleasure or excitement from anything. If you believe you can't be happy without it, you won't. With the willpower method, you never properly remove this belief.

WHEN YOU NO LONGER HAVE THE DESIRE FOR JUNK FOOD, YOU DON'T REGARD IT AS A TREAT. YOU DON'T MISS IT BECAUSE IT MAKES NO CONTRIBUTION TO YOUR ENJOYMENT. IN FACT, IT NEVER DID

The brainwashing causes addicts to have a romanticized idea of their "drug." Usually the things they think they'll miss are situations they haven't even experienced for real. Where there have been enjoyable situations involving junk food, a quick analysis of all the details of that situation will reveal that there were other aspects that made it enjoyable: The presence of friends, an exciting location, a celebration of some kind, and so on.

If you have occasions like this that you considered enjoyable because you were eating junk, analyse them carefully to understand why the food appeared to enhance the situation and see that in reality it was more likely to do the opposite. Instead of maintaining the illusion that such occasions won't be enjoyable again without junk food, take the opposite view; remind yourself you will now be able to enjoy those occasions more because you'll be free from the slavery of emotional eating.

Most of the time you're not even aware of how you feel while you're eating junk. The only time you're really aware is when you want it but can't have it, or when you're eating it but wish you weren't. In both cases, it makes you miserable. The conclusion is obvious:

TAKE AWAY THE JUNK FOOD AND YOU REMOVE THE MISERY

WILL I BE ABLE TO ENDURE THE BAD TIMES?

This question is just as important, if not more so. Emotional eating is mostly triggered by negative emotions and the need for comfort.

There are many situations that can send you running to the cupboard: a family row, work pressure, financial problems, a trauma... You can take yourself out of the situation, focus on the food, and put your problems out of your mind.

But sooner or later you have to return to the real world and the problems are still there. In fact, they've usually gotten worse. If you believe that junk food provides comfort in these situations, you leave yourself vulnerable after you've quit. The next time you feel the need for comfort, the Big Monster pulls you back into the trap.

Think about it: How is food going to help you with any of the problems in your life? Have you ever found yourself in the middle of a domestic row thinking, "It doesn't matter that we're shouting horrible, hurtful things at each other because I can just go and eat a box of cookies and it will be all right"?

Or did the fact that you ate too many cookies make you feel worse?

Everyone has stressful situations in life, but not everyone is left moping because they can't eat junk. All you have to do is accept that you will have ups and downs in your life after you've quit and understand that if you start yearning for junk in such situations, you'll be moping for an illusion and opening up a void.

EMOTIONAL EATING REDUCES YOUR ABILITY TO COPE WITH STRESSFUL SITUATIONS BY ADDING TO THE STRESS

Even when you're completely clear about this, it's possible to feel confused when hard times occur and you find yourself feeling low again. That familiar feeling can make a former addict think they're falling back into the trap.

You can avoid this potential pitfall by anticipating the difficult times that will inevitably occur after you've quit and prepare yourself mentally. Remind yourself that any stress you feel is not because you can't eat junk. Tell yourself, "OK, this is tough, but at least I don't have the added problem of being a slave to emotional eating. I am stronger now."

You will find that the stressful situations in your life will actually feel less severe once you are free from emotional eating.

BEING FREE ENHANCES ALL SITUATIONS IN LIFE—GOOD AND BAD

THE MOMENT OF REVELATION

Soon you will be ready to go through a ritual, which I call "the final feast." It doesn't have to be a feast, but it will be a final reminder of the grim reality of emotional eating. Afterward, you will be able to say you are no longer addicted to junk food; you have no desire for it; you are free from emotional eating.

The purpose of this ritual is to draw a line in the sand: The point at which you walked free from the trap. This is not necessarily the moment when you realize you are free. That can happen beforehand. You may even have reached that point already.

When you've been trapped in a prison for a long time and then the door suddenly swings open, you may sit and savor the moment for a while before walking out.

The final feast is the act of walking out of the prison, discovering that your perception of the world around you really has changed, and beginning your new life of freedom.

When you achieve something big, like passing an exam, landing a job, or winning a competition, you experience a wonderful high as the realization of your achievement sinks in. A lot of people feel the same thing when they quit with Easyway—a moment of revelation. The confusion caused by addiction is suddenly replaced by absolute clarity and understanding—a thrilling realization that their desire for junk food has gone.

This clarity is essential. It is not enough to *try* or *hope* that you will never get hooked again; you must be certain. Easyway is designed to give you that certainty.

Unlike the willpower method, Easyway doesn't leave you waiting for some sign of confirmation that you are free. You won't spend the rest of your life suspecting that there could be bad news lurking just around the corner.

YOU KNOW YOU'RE FREE THE MOMENT YOU
EXPERIENCE THE MOMENT OF REVELATION

Chapter 15

YOU ARE NOT ALONE

Emotional eating is a lonely condition that can leave you feeling that you're the only one with the problem. It's important that you can see that you are not alone with it and that, however you go about fueling your addiction, the instructions for quitting apply to you in exactly the same way as they do for everybody else.

Emotional eating comes in as many forms as there are uncomfortable emotions.

It's possible to regard yourself as different from all other emotional eaters and this in turn could lead you to suspect that Easyway might not be able to help you. Let me stress this very clearly:

ALL EMOTIONAL EATERS HAVE THE SAME PROBLEM

Easyway is the proven method for tackling that problem. If you choose to believe that you are beyond the help of Easyway, all you will do is insure that you remain in the trap. The only reason for choosing to remain in the trap is the fear of success. If you haven't yet overcome the fear of success, go back and read Chapter 7. It's essential that you remove any doubts over your decision to quit.

SECRET EATERS

Secret eaters spend their lives living a lie. Not only do they lie to themselves that they get some pleasure or comfort from eating junk food, they also lie to other people that they don't eat junk food at all! They are so ashamed of it that they go to great lengths to hide it from anyone else.

Constantly having to cover your tracks is highly stressful and can lead to higher and higher risks. It also takes a heavy toll on your self-respect, which only compounds any feelings of loneliness and anxiety.

All emotional eaters are secret eaters to some extent. Emotional eating requires you to lie to yourself because there is no logic to it. You know it makes no sense. You wish you could stop and don't understand why you can't. If you owned up to the full extent of your problem, you would have to admit that there is no pleasure or comfort in it, but you can't do that because it's the only reason you have for carrying on.

One of the greatest pleasures of escaping the trap is never having to lie to yourself again. The sense of freedom from all the deceit and slavery is amazing.

WOMEN AND MEN

There's a general perception that emotional eating is a problem for women. Most of the newspaper and magazine articles you read about it take a female angle and show pictures of women. But men are exposed to the same brainwashing from birth and suffer from emotional eating too.

There is a difference in how the pressures and preconceptions of eating junk food affect men and women. Historically, until more recent, enlightened times, women have been expected to take more care of their figure, to watch what they eat, and to exercise more self-control. For men, by contrast, overeating has been more socially acceptable. Men go to extremes; men overindulge; men have pot bellies.

But society is beginning to realize that men also suffer from emotional eating problems. Being overweight is no more fun for a man than it is for a woman. Putting weight to one side, losing control of your diet, binge-eating, wishing you could stop but feeling powerless to change is miserable and unnerving for both sexes.

There's a real stigma attached to emotional eating and, regardless of gender, sufferers feel more compelled to cover it up and do their eating in secret. At the same time, the pressures on everyone today are greater than ever and the compulsion to find comfort in food has risen accordingly.

The important point is that your emotional eating problem has nothing to do with whether you're a woman or a man. The illusions that keep you in the trap are the same for everybody.

As you unravel the brainwashing, it's also worth noticing how the junk food industry targets specific groups. Some products are aimed at women; some are aimed at men. Be aware that you are being very specifically targeted and if you find yourself hooked on a particular type of junk food, invariably that's because someone has made the decision to hook you. The junk food industry, and I include supermarkets in that category, is one of the most sophisticated and merciless marketing machines on the planet.

You don't turn to food because you're weak, or addictive, or ill-disciplined, or whatever. It's not a flaw in your character or DNA. It's because there's a Big Monster in your brain that feeds you false messages every time you feel the slightest emotional need.

PICKERS AND CHOOSERS

Some people seem to be able to eat junk whenever they feel like it without ever becoming a slave to it. These people can hamper your efforts to quit by making you feel that you're different and that your problem is beyond control. In fact, these pickers and choosers are no more in control of their eating than you are. They still believe that junk food gives them pleasure or comfort. For whatever reasons—for example, a less stressful lifestyle—they just don't feel the need as strongly as you do.

No doubt you've come across the old adage, "A little of what you fancy does you good." It means that it's safe for you to indulge in anything that might be bad for you, provided you don't do it to excess.

Physically speaking, there is some truth in this. I've talked about the human body as an incredible machine with the remarkable ability to recover from dietary abuse. Eating a cream cake once in a while might not kill you, but then it won't do you any good either. Extend the argument to smoking and other drugs and you start to feel more uneasy about having "a little of what you fancy." Would you say to someone you care about, "Try a shot of heroin, just a little won't hurt you?"

There are two main reasons why ex-addicts get hooked again. One is that they never completely removed the brainwashing, and so there remains a lingering sense of deprivation. The other is that they reach a point where they are so confident that they have overcome their addiction that they decide they can have the occasional fix without getting hooked again.

The fact that they want that fix shows that they have not removed the brainwashing either. The cycle of addiction is just waiting to start all over again. All emotional eaters wish they could eat less, and so they envy pickers and choosers. They appear to be in control, but this is an illusion. They are constantly fighting the cycle of addiction.

They know deep down that eating junk food doesn't give them pleasure or comfort; otherwise why not do it all the time? At the same time, they're not convinced that they can live happily without it; otherwise they would leave it out completely.

If you believe there is an idyllic alternative to being either a non-junk food eater or a junk food addict who's hooked for life—a happy casual junk food eater—let me ask you a simple question: Why are you not one already?

If I said I could fix it so that you could eat junk just once a week for the rest of your life, would you accept it? Better still, suppose I told you you could control things, so that you ate junk only when you really wanted to? That's a pretty exciting offer, isn't it?

But that's what you already do!

Has anyone ever forced you to eat junk? Isn't it more the case that you've always eaten junk because you wanted to, even though part of your brain wished you didn't?

The fact is that these casual bingers are creating a number of serious problems for themselves:

1. They keep themselves addicted to junk food.

2. They wish their lives away waiting for the next fix.

3. Instead of relieving the craving whenever they feel like it, they force themselves to endure the discomfort, and so are permanently restless.

4. They reinforce the illusion that eating junk food is a pleasure or comfort.

You might think it sounds nice to only feel the urge to eat junk every now and then. Wouldn't it be nicer to never want to do it at all? The reason you do it more often than you would like to is because you're not happy doing it less. As long as you believe that it gives you pleasure or comfort, the natural urge is to do it more. But doing it more makes you miserable too. That's the fiendish ingenuity of the trap: As long as you're in it, it doesn't matter whether you do it more or less often, you become increasingly miserable either way.

THE ONLY WAY TO BE HAPPY IS TO STOP SEEKING PLEASURE OR COMFORT IN JUNK FOOD ALTOGETHER

CUTTING DOWN AND USING SUBSTITUTES

When you quit with the willpower method, the standard approach is to gradually reduce your intake rather than stopping at once. The theory is that you give your body the chance to adjust to smaller and smaller doses until it's just a short step to stopping completely.

At the same time, you will be advised to use substitutes to help you through the withdrawal period: Methadone for heroin addicts, patches and gum or e-cigarettes for smokers, sweeteners for sugar addicts.

Easyway is different. There is no cutting down and there is no need for substitutes. I devised the method this way for one simple reason:

CUTTING DOWN AND USING SUBSTITUTES DOESN'T WORK

I knew that from my many failed attempts to quit smoking. Believe me, I tried everything. I could cut down, but I could never get completely free and I would always end up falling back deeper into the trap than before. The less I smoked, the more I craved cigarettes. I found it baffling and hugely frustrating, but after I had my moment of revelation and understood the nature of addiction, it became abundantly obvious.

Cutting down is counter-productive to getting permanently free from addiction for two reasons:

1. It increases the value you place on your little fix.

2. It weakens your resolve to quit.

Cutting down increases the illusion of pleasure because the longer you endure the craving, the greater the sense of pleasure when you relieve that craving. If you think increasing the illusion of pleasure sounds like a good thing, think again. The only way to increase the illusion of pleasure is to increase the aggravation.

It's like wearing tighter and tighter shoes in order to get increasing relief from taking them off. No one enjoys the aggravation of being a junk food addict. There is a constant impulse to scratch the itch and the more you scratch it, the worse it gets.

That's why cutting down is unsustainable and usually results in you eating more junk than before.

Substitutes are also counter-productive for two big reasons:

1. They perpetuate the myth that withdrawal is an ordeal.

2. They keep the Big Monster alive and make you feel deprived.

We will look more closely at withdrawal in the next chapter. The key thing to remember is that it's not your body that needs help in getting free; it's your mind. The only way to free your mind from the tyranny of addiction is to kill the Big Monster.

As you will soon discover, this is a marvelous moment. You will know immediately that you're free and the idea of cutting down will be ridiculous. Why attempt to crawl out of the prison when you can take one triumphant step?

Chapter 16

WITHDRAWAL

One of the myths that hold addicts back from trying to quit is that the process will be hard and painful, but like so many aspects of addiction, the fear of the withdrawal period is founded on false assumptions. When you quit with Easyway, the withdrawal symptoms become a source of pleasure, not a pain.

Withdrawal is an interesting word. We associate it with quitting, but, in fact, it is something that is part and parcel of the repetitive cycle of addiction. Every time you eat junk food it triggers withdrawal pangs as the initial boost subsides and the effects wear off, leaving an empty, restless feeling.

It is the need to soothe this empty, restless feeling that makes you think about your next fix.

Physically the feeling is so slight that you can hardly feel it. This is the Little Monster. Keep your mind occupied with something else and you can easily get by completely unaware of the feeling. But the feeling awakes the Big Monster in your brain, and this is when the urge to satisfy the craving becomes hard to resist.

So when you fear that quitting will be hard because you'll have to go through the ordeal of withdrawal, what you're actually fearing is a tiny sensation that you already feel several times a day and that amounts to nothing more than a slight itch. Withdrawal from Bad Sugar addiction is barely noticeable; it only becomes unpleasant if it triggers the Big Monster and if you start moping after emotional eating.

THE PANIC

Most emotional eaters are familiar with the "panic" feeling that sets in when you feel the pangs of withdrawal and you don't know when you'll next get the opportunity to eat junk. Many go to great lengths to insure this never happens, keeping well stocked with snacks and sweets.

The result, of course, is that the determination to avoid withdrawal drives you deeper into the trap faster. You don't wait between fixes; it becomes a continuous process, like chain smoking. This helps to explain the earlier question about why some people become more hooked than others. The fear of withdrawal speeds up the cycle of addiction.

Withdrawal is not painful, but if you're afraid that it will be you will do whatever you can to avoid it. It's the fear of pain that causes the panic, not actual pain. Because there is no actual pain.

This might go against things you've read elsewhere. You can look online and quickly find lists of withdrawal symptoms that would make you think twice about trying to quit. Symptoms such as:

• Tiredness

• Headaches

• Stomach upsets

• Weak and aching muscles

• Heart palpitations

• The shakes

• The sweats

• The shivers

• Difficulty breathing

People who quit with Easyway don't experience these symptoms. They are all symptoms of chronic anxiety and are caused by the mental panic brought on by the fear of withdrawal and the feeling of missing out on something that might be pleasurable or supportive to you. In other words:

THE FEAR OF WITHDRAWAL PAINS IS SELF-FULFILLING

But, say you do experience those symptoms. Is that really something to fear? They are very similar to the symptoms of flu. No doubt you've had flu before and you probably expect to get it again. Flu is horrible, but does the thought of getting flu make you panic? You know you can withstand it. Is it not worth going through a short bout of flu to get free of your addiction to junk?

In fact, you're very well equipped to withstand a high degree of pain. You can try it for yourself. Squeeze your fingernails into your forearm and gradually increase the pressure. You'll find you can endure quite a severe level of pain without any sense of fear or panic. That's because you're in control. You know what's causing the pain, and you know that you can make it stop whenever you choose.

But if you started feeling a pain like that in your forearm and didn't know what was causing it or how bad it was going to get, you would start to panic. Pain is not the problem; the problem is the fear and panic that pain induces if you don't understand why you're feeling it or what the consequences might be. In fact, we often panic at the slightest feeling of discomfort if we don't know what's caused it and fear it might be the beginning of something severe.

Observe any type of addict when they're denied their fix. They'll be restless and fidgety. You'll notice little nervous tics; they'll be constantly doing things with their hands or grinding their teeth. This restlessness is triggered by an empty, insecure feeling that can quickly turn into frustration, irritability, anxiety, anger, fear, and panic.

Get it clear in your mind that eating junk food causes this feeling; it doesn't relieve it. As long as you understand that, you don't need to feel any sense of panic when you stop.

When you quit with Easyway, it's easy to get through the withdrawal period because you know that the empty, restless feeling is caused by eating junk food and that it will soon pass. You also know that the one thing that will insure you suffer that feeling for the rest of your life is to keep eating junk.

Rather than panicking, you will experience a wonderful feeling of freedom.

ENJOY WITHDRAWAL

After you've completed the ritual of the Final Feast, you will continue to experience the withdrawal craving for a few days. Remember, this is not a physical pain, it's just the faint cries of the Little Monster wanting to be fed. You could easily ignore it, but please don't.

This is the time to keep in mind the fact that the Little Monster was created when you first started eating junk and it has continued to feed on every subsequent bit of junk food you've had. As soon as you stop, you cut off the food supply and that vile Little Monster begins to die.

In its death throes, it will try to entice you to feed it. Create a mental image of this parasite getting weaker and weaker and enjoy starving it to death. Remember, it's the Little Monster that will be starving, not you. If you experience genuine hunger, you'll eat something but not junk. If you feel that emotional eating Little Monster, you can smile to yourself and brush it away as if it were a little piece of lint on your shoulder.

Keep this mental image with you at all times and make sure you don't respond to its death throes by lapsing into thinking, "I'd like a snack." Remember that that would only prolong the feeling.

Take a sadistic delight in feeling the Little Monster die. Even if you do get that feeling of "I'd like a snack" for a few days, don't worry about it. It's just the Little Monster doing everything it can to tempt you. Without the Big Monster, it's powerless and you will find it easy to keep starving it.

WHEN CAN I RELAX?

You're probably thinking, "OK, but how long will this go on for? I can't keep this up 24/7."

The point is you can start enjoying the genuine pleasure of no longer being an emotional eater from the moment you kill the Big Monster. Unlike the willpower method, with Easyway you don't have to wait for anything *not* to happen.

It usually takes a few days for the physical withdrawal to pass. Then, after about three weeks, there comes a moment when you suddenly realize that you haven't thought about eating junk food for a while. If you quit with the willpower method, this is a dangerous moment. You feel great. You feel powerful. You feel in control. It's time to celebrate. What possible harm could it do to reward yourself just a little? But the Big Monster is not dead. Sooner or later, it will drag you back into the trap.

With Easyway, however, you will not feel that you've made a sacrifice, and so you won't feel like celebrating by eating junk again. You can relax from the moment you complete your Final Feast and realize that the desire has gone. Instead of responding to the withdrawal pangs by thinking, "I'd like a snack," you think, "Yes! I'm free. I don't ever have to go through that misery again."

NO GET-OUT CLAUSE

Some addicts, once they realize that it's just fear that prevents them from stopping, try to allay that fear by telling themselves they can always start again if it gets too hard—that quitting doesn't have to be final.

If you start off with that attitude, you're very likely to fail sooner or later. Instead, start off with the certainty that you're going to be free forever. To achieve that certainty, you have to remove the fear and panic first.

Chapter 17

TAKING CONTROL

IN THIS CHAPTER

• *ESCAPE FROM SLAVERY* • *THE CHOICE IS YOURS*
• *PAYING ATTENTION* • *KILLING THE BIG MONSTER*
• *PREPARE YOUR MIND* • *SHARE THE GOOD NEWS*

There are many painful aspects to emotional eating. The most painful of all is the feeling that you are not in control. The aim of this book is not just to help you overcome your emotional eating problem but to be able to enjoy food and feel in control of what you eat and when. It's not the restricted, disciplined, craving kind of control that you've had to exercise for so long as an emotional eater; it's free and easy knowing that you can eat your favorite foods. The time to reclaim control, to escape from slavery, has arrived.

When it comes to the reasons emotional eaters give for wanting to quit, weight is the most common answer. Losing your figure, losing fitness, becoming obese, developing diabetes—these effects and risks cause stress and misery, and that in itself is a very good reason to stop.

The social effects of overeating are also a common reason for wanting to quit. Social isolation is a major threat for emotional eaters. The shame and secrecy can drive you into a self-inflicted form of solitary confinement. The effect on your moods and behavior, and how that affects family and friends, can be devastating and if you're fortunate enough to recognize it before it's too late, then this too can provide all the incentive you need to quit.

Ask an emotional eater why they eat junk and they will nearly always react defensively and negatively. They can't seem to find positive reasons why they do, but resort to excuses for why they haven't stopped yet.

"Oh, I'm just a chocaholic"

"You can't live your whole life on greens"

"What's the point of living if you can't have the odd binge?"

These are very different from the sort of answers you get if you ask someone why they play baseball, or go to the movies, or visit art galleries, or listen to music. When something gives you genuine pleasure, you're only too eager to enthuse about it. You don't make excuses for why you don't stop doing it! Defensiveness is a sure sign of someone who knows they are not in control.

Although you are constantly bombarded with misinformation designed to make you eat junk, all emotional eaters are aware of the many good reasons not to. Your attempts to stop or cut down are driven by one or more of these reasons, but it's only when you succeed in stopping that you realize the greatest gain to be had from quitting:

ESCAPE FROM SLAVERY

When you're an emotional eater, the temptation to eat junk is so great that you find any flimsy excuse that will allow you to keep doing so and shut down to the logic of quitting.

Though you know and hate the fact that you're not in control, you refuse to confront the slavery.

Addicts don't like to think of themselves as slaves. The heaviest addicts tend to be very strong-willed people who have enjoyed a high degree of control over most of their lives and it irritates them to think that they are being controlled by something for which they have no respect.

This is what makes us believe that we should be able to conquer our addictions through sheer force of will—and leaves us depressed and short-tempered when we can't.

The key that enables addicts to get free is the realization that their days of slavery are over:

- You no longer need to be a slave to food that does absolutely nothing for you

- You won't miss it

- You will enjoy life more

- You will be able to deal better with stress

- You won't have to go through some terrible trauma in order to escape.

THE CHOICE IS YOURS

Every emotional eater chooses to eat junk. Nobody forces you to do it. Every time you eat a cake or cookie, you are exercising your own personal choice. But how can someone who is not in control exercise a choice?

When you're addicted, you are not in control, yet you constantly feel exhausted and frustrated by your attempts to stay in control, and yet you are still the one making the decision to eat junk. All addicts are controlled into thinking that they are making choices that are good for them. They weigh up what they know about the risks against their beliefs about the hardship of quitting and make a choice that it's better to stay in the trap.

It's a choice they hate themselves for making, yet the alternative is worse, or so they've been led to believe.

This constant wrestle between logic and illusion is what goes on in every addict's mind. It's confusing and makes you feel foolish and pathetic. Nobody likes to feel that way, so you go into denial; you bury your head in the sand in order to avoid the painful truth about what you've become: A hopeless, pathetic slave to junk food. Instead of facing up to this unpleasant reality and doing the one thing that will free you—stop eating junk—you search for excuses to keep doing it.

Only when you face up to your situation and admit that you've become a slave can you escape from the trap. In order to take control, you have to recognize and understand that junk food controls you, not the other way around, and that it is not the solution to your misery but the cause.

PAYING ATTENTION

Enjoying the withdrawal pangs is part of the process of taking control. The cries of the Little Monster no longer make you react by thinking,

"I'd like a snack", they make you think, "Great, the Little Monster is suffering and will soon die. I'm winning."

Your first positive step in taking control of your emotional eating problem was choosing to read this book. You had a choice: To bury your head in the sand and continue stumbling further and further into the trap, or to take positive action to resolve the situation. You made a positive choice. That might seem like a long way back now. Keep making those positive choices and you will soon experience the moment of revelation.

As we approach the Final Feast, there are three very important facts that I want you to remember:

1. Junk food does absolutely nothing for you at all.
It is crucial that you understand why this is so and accept it, so that you never get a feeling of deprivation.

2. There is no need for a gradual transition.
With drug addicts this is often referred to as the "withdrawal period." But anyone who quits with Easyway has no need to worry about the withdrawal period. Yes, it may take time to repair the damage caused by your overeating, but the moment you stop believing that you need junk food for pleasure or comfort is the moment you become free. You don't have to wait for anything *not* to happen.

3. There is no such thing as "just this once" or "the occasional binge."
If you're still tempted to eat junk, the Big Monster is still alive. You have to remove any desire to eat junk, which means understanding and believing the fact that it does absolutely nothing for you whatsoever.

Don't be worried if the thought of eating junk pops into your head—
as long as you react by smiling and enjoying your feeling of freedom,
that's fine.

KILLING THE BIG MONSTER

It's bizarre but many addicts suffer from the delusion that life wouldn't
be complete without their addiction. They convince themselves that
it is their friend, their confidence, their support, even part of their
identity. And so they fear that if they quit, they will not only lose their
closest companion, they will lose a part of themselves.

It's a stark indication of just how severely the brainwashing distorts
reality, that anyone should come to regard something that is destroying
them and making them miserable as a friend.

When you lose a friend, you grieve. Eventually you come to terms
with the loss and life goes on, but you're left with a genuine void in
your life that you can never fill. There's nothing you can do about
it. You have no choice but to accept the situation and, though it still
hurts, you do.

When addicts try to quit by using willpower, they feel like they're
losing a friend. They know that they're making the right decision to
stop, but they still suffer a sense of loss and, therefore, there's a void
in their lives. They feel as if they're mourning for a friend, yet this
false friend isn't even dead. The temptation of forbidden fruit stays
with them for the rest of their lives—the purveyors of junk food make
absolutely sure of that. Can you imagine moping after that thief who
pretended to be a friend, so they could steal from you? They didn't
just steal from you though, they humiliated you, and laughed at your
expense. You'd never feel anything but contempt for them once you
found out the truth about them.

When you rid yourself of your mortal enemy—the Big Monster that makes you believe that you need junk food—there is no reason to mourn. On the contrary, you can rejoice and celebrate from the start, and you can continue to rejoice and celebrate for the rest of your life.

That's why it's vital to get it clear in your mind that junk food is not your friend, nor is it part of your identity. It never has been. In fact, it's your mortal enemy and by getting rid of it you're sacrificing nothing, just making marvelous, positive gains.

I don't need to convince you of this in writing. When you kill the Big Monster, you will instantly know it for yourself.

So the answer to the question, "When will I be free?" is "Whenever you choose to be." You could spend the next few days, and possibly the rest of your life, continuing to believe that junk food was your friend and wondering when you'll stop missing it. If you do that, you will feel miserable; the desire for junk may never leave you, and you'll either end up feeling deprived for the rest of your life, or you'll end up falling back into the trap and feeling even worse.

Alternatively, you can recognize junk food for the mortal enemy that it really is and take pleasure in cutting it out of your life. Then you need never crave it again and, whenever it enters your mind, you will feel elated that it is no longer ruining your life.

Unlike people who quit with the willpower method, you'll be happy to think about your old enemy and you needn't try to block it from your mind. In fact, it's important that you don't. Trying not to think about something is a sure way of becoming obsessed with it. For example, if I tell you not to think about elephants, what's the first thing that comes into your head?

Exactly!

There's no reason to try not to think about eating junk. You are now in control again and are free to enjoy thinking about your old enemy and rejoice that it no longer plagues your life.

Soon I am going to ask you to perform the ritual of the Final Feast. Once you've done so, you will find it easy never to seek pleasure or comfort in junk food again or to eat in response to emotions rather than hunger. And once you realize that you have the power to stop, you will feel a wonderful sense of freedom.

REAL FREEDOM

PREPARE YOUR MIND

You might find that, particularly during the first few days, you forget that you've quit. It can happen at any time. You think, "I'll have a snack." Then you remember you don't do that any more. But you wonder why the thought entered your head when you were convinced you'd killed the Big Monster.

Such times can be crucial in whether you succeed or not. React in the wrong way and they can be disastrous. Doubts can surface and you may start to question your decision to quit and lose faith in yourself.

Prepare for these situations so that you remain calm and, instead of thinking, "I can't do it," think, "Isn't it great! I don't need to eat junk anymore. I'm free!" Brush it away as if it was a tiny piece of lint on your shoulder.

Remember too that you will still be prone to feeling genuine hunger, especially if you follow my advice about paying attention to your hunger gauge. True hunger is an empty, restless feeling similar to the cries of the Little Monster. Be prepared so that you don't confuse them.

Even without the Big Monster to drive you toward junk food, your old routine can trip you up and you might find yourself looking for a junk food fix before you realize what you're doing.

If this happens, don't panic. It doesn't mean the Big Monster is still alive; it just means that you're subconsciously following your old routine. Take pleasure in remembering that you no longer need to do that, be aware of your hunger and satisfy it with something genuinely satisfying.

If you momentarily forget that you no longer eat junk, that isn't a bad sign; it's a very good one. It's proof that your life is returning to the happy state you were in before you got hooked, when emotional eating didn't dominate your whole existence.

Expecting these moments to happen and being prepared for them means you won't be caught off guard. You'll be wearing a suit of impregnable armor. You know you've made the correct decision and nobody will be able to make you doubt it. That way, instead of being the cause of your downfall, these moments can give you strength, security, and immense pleasure, reminding you just how wonderful it is to be...

FREE!

SHARE THE GOOD NEWS

Being real and honest about your problem is the surest sign that you're regaining control. You have been honest with yourself by taking the decision to read this book. Why not share your situation with anyone you've been hiding it from?

Perhaps you find the idea of owning up unthinkable. You are afraid that people will lose respect for you. It's far more likely that they will respect you for your honesty and will support you all the way. Covering up your addiction is immensely stressful and damages your self-respect.

It's also more than likely that the people you think you've been deceiving haven't been deceived at all when you were addicted.

Don't be surprised to find that they are relieved by your admission. If you really would like to keep your freedom private, then by all means do. Do whatever you feel you want to in order to feel comfortable.

You will be amazed by how good it feels to be free from the slavery of emotional eating. The benefits are enormous:

- More time for work and play

- A greater ability to concentrate

- A greater ability to cope with stress

- Being able to enjoy genuine pleasures again

- A healthier lifestyle

- A sharper, brighter, happier state of mind

- Real control over your life

Your moment to take control and escape from the emotional eating trap has arrived.

Congratulations! You deserve to be feeling very excited. Enjoy the process of escape.

Look forward to all the benefits you are about to receive. And whenever the thought of eating junk enters your mind, don't feel miserable because you can't. Think, "YIPPEE! I don't have to do that any more. I'm FREE!"

Chapter 18

THE FINAL FEAST

IN THIS CHAPTER
- *CHECK YOUR MINDSET* • *CHOOSING YOUR MOMENT*
- *THE FINAL FEAST* • *DON'T WAIT FOR THE OUTCOME*

The time has come to complete your escape. Your mind is right, you have all the information you need, and a life of happy, healthy eating awaits you. All that's left to do is to mark the occasion with a ritual that will stay with you forever.

So here you are. You've reached the moment of truth. If you've followed all the instructions, you should by now be feeling eager and excited about becoming an ex-emotional eater. Today's the day!

Your frame of mind should be completely different from how it was when you first picked up the book. You've reversed the brainwashing and dispelled the illusions that made you believe that eating junk food gave you pleasure and comfort. You've replaced them with the truth: Junk food does absolutely nothing for you whatsoever.

You've discovered that rather than being a real friend, that gave you support and pleasure, instead you've uncovered a thief, someone who stole from you and treated you with contempt.

It's time to celebrate. You are about to walk free from a fiendish trap that has kept you imprisoned and miserable, threatened your health and happiness, and left you feeling helpless like a slave. You have now reclaimed control over your life and those feelings of slavery and helplessness should have been banished for good. You know you have the power to quit.

Take pride in your achievement; there isn't an emotional eater in the world who wouldn't wish they could be in your shoes. You are about to discover the unbridled joy of having nothing to hide, having time and energy for the people you love and the things you love to do. Addiction makes you lose touch with the genuine pleasures in life. You're about to get that huge part of your life back.

Give yourself a big pat on the back

If this *isn't* how you feel, if you have doubts about what you are about to do, it means that you haven't understood something I've told you and you need to go back and re-read it until you do. To help you spot any gaps in your understanding, take a look at the code word, RATIONALIZED, opposite. This serves as both a reminder and a checklist. Go through each item and ask yourself:

- Do I understand it?

- Do I agree with it?

- Am I following it?

If you have any doubts, reread the relevant chapters as listed.

R REJOICE!

You're freeing yourself from a tyrant. (See Chapter 3)

A ADVICE

Ignore it if it conflicts with Easyway. (See Chapter 10)

T TIMING

Do it now! (See this chapter)

I IMMEDIATE

You don't have to wait for anything *not* to happen. (See Chapter 17)

O ONE BINGE

Is all it takes to hook you again. (See Chapter 15)

N NEVER

Seek pleasure or comfort from junk food. (See Chapters 12 and 13)

A ADDICTIVE PERSONALITY

There's no such thing. (See Chapter 9)

L LIFESTYLE

Rediscover genuine pleasures. (See Chapters 17 and 19)

I INCREMENTAL CURES

Cutting down and using substitutes keep you trapped. (See Chapters 15 and 16)

Z ZEAL

You have new favorite foods to enthuse over. (See Chapter 3)

E ELEPHANTS

Don't try not to think about eating junk. (See Chapter 17)

D DOUBT

Never doubt your decision to quit. (See Chapter 7)

Stopping with Easyway is not difficult. All you need to do is follow the instructions and you will succeed. You have already done the work that was necessary to put yourself in the right frame of mind. You have opened your mind to ideas that previously seemed far-fetched and now you know the truth.

JUNK FOOD DOESN'T GIVE YOU PLEASURE OR COMFORT; IT DOES ABSOLUTELY NOTHING FOR YOU WHATSOEVER. THE ONLY REASON YOU USED TO THINK IT DOES IS BECAUSE YOU'D BEEN BRAINWASHED AND ADDICTED TO BAD SUGAR

You have been given everything you need to succeed at something that other ex-emotional eaters regard as the most important and significant achievement of their lives. If you feel like a dog straining at the leash, eager to get on with it, that's great, but you still need to concentrate carefully on the rest of the book.

If you are clear on all the points in the RATIONALIZED list and have followed and understood all the instructions, then you should be feeling the relief of knowing that the Big Monster has been destroyed.

If you haven't had an amazing moment of revelation, don't worry. The realization dawns on different people in different ways; don't wait for it to happen. In a day or so, or a few days, or a week, it'll suddenly dawn on you: You're free. The important thing is that the Big Monster is dead. If you are confident of that then you are ready for the ritual of the Final Feast. You may be wondering when would be the ideal moment.

CHOOSING YOUR MOMENT

Picking your moment to quit is a common dilemma for all addicts. The tendency is to choose an occasion that represents a milestone of some kind. These milestones typically fall into two types: a traumatic event, such as a health scare; or a "special" day, such as a birthday or New Year's Day.

These "special" days actually have no bearing whatsoever on your problem, other than providing a target date for you to begin your attempt to stop. I call them "meaningless days." It would be perfectly OK if they helped, but meaningless days actually cause much more harm than good.

New Year's Day is the most popular of all meaningless days, being a clear marker of the end of one period and the beginning of another. It also happens to have the lowest success rate. The Christmas holidays are a time when we eat to excess and by New Year's Eve we're just about ready for a break.

So you make a decision to cut out the junk and after a few days you're feeling cleansed. But the Little Monster is screaming for its fix. If you're using the wrong method and don't understand that, far from solving the problem, eating junk will make it worse, you give in to the Little Monster's cries.

Meaningless days only encourage you to go through the damaging cycle of half-hearted attempts to quit, bringing on the feeling of deprivation, followed by the sense of failure that reinforces the belief that stopping is very difficult. Emotional eaters spend their lives looking for excuses to put off "the dreaded day." Meaningless days provide the perfect excuse to say, "I will quit, just not today."

That said, if you happen to be reading this on New Year's Day or any other "meaningless day," don't worry; with Easyway, you'll escape in spite of the day rather than because of it.

Then there are the days when some trauma shakes your world and you respond by saying it's time to sort yourself out. But these stressful times are also when your desire to comfort eat becomes strongest.

This is another ingenuity of the trap:

NO MATTER WHICH DAY YOU CHOOSE TO QUIT, IT ALWAYS SEEMS TO BE WRONG

Some people choose their annual vacation to quit, thinking that they'll be able to cope better away from the everyday stresses of work and home life and the usual temptations. Others pick a time when there are no big events coming up that might entice them to binge. These approaches might work for a while, but they leave a lingering doubt: "OK, I've coped so far, but what about when I go back to work or that big party comes up?"

When you quit with Easyway, you are encouraged to go out and handle stress and throw yourself into social occasions straightaway. This way you can prove to yourself from the start that, even at times when you feared you would find it hard to cope, you're still happy to be free.

So what is the best time to quit? Let's go back to the door analogy from Chapter 8. When you're stuck in the trap, trying to will yourself free, it's like trying to open a door by pushing on the side where the hinges are, rather than the side with the handle. If you'd been pushing fruitlessly on the wrong side of a door and then you discovered you could open it easily by pushing on the other side, would you wait until New Year's Day? Or until your birthday? Or until you went on vacation? Or would you make your move there and then?

Don't waste time thinking about the best time to stop. There is only one logical answer…

DO IT NOW!

You have everything you need to quit. Like an athlete on the blocks at the start of the Olympic 100 meters final, you are in peak condition to make the greatest achievement of your life RIGHT NOW!

Think of everything you have to gain. A life free from slavery, dishonesty, misery, anger, deceit, self-loathing, helplessness.

No more wasting your money on junk; no more covering up; no more worrying about your health; no more missing out on genuine pleasures; no more wanting to stop but feeling powerless to resist. Those days are gone as soon as you decide to make your move.

In their place, you can look forward to living in the light with your head held high, enjoying open, honest relationships with the people around you, feeling in control of how you spend your time and money, enjoying eating again, and rediscovering the other genuine pleasures that you enjoyed before you became an emotional eater. You'll recognize the real YOU!

With so much happiness to gain and so much misery to shed, what possible reason is there to wait?

EIGHTH INSTRUCTION:
DON'T WAIT FOR THE RIGHT TIME TO QUIT; DO IT NOW!

THE FINAL FEAST

At the start of this journey I asked you not to change your diet. I wanted you to keep eating as usual right up to the point where you were ready to quit for good. This wasn't because junk food provides any sort of benefit; it was because addicts who are deprived of their fix become fixated. I needed you to follow my method without any distractions.

You are now ready to take your final step to freedom and make the change from being an emotional eater to being a happy, healthy eater.

The ritual of the Final Feast is important for several reasons. This is a momentous occasion in your life and one of the most important decisions you will ever make. You are freeing yourself from slavery and achieving something marvelous. It deserves to be marked with some ceremony. The ritual will give you something positive to relate back to should the memory of how good you feel begin to fade.

The most important purpose of the ritual, though, is this: The thing that makes it difficult to quit is not the physical aggravation of withdrawal; it's the doubt, the uncertainty, the waiting to become cured. With Easyway, you become a happy, healthy eater the moment you complete your Final Feast. It is not a gradual process; it is a moment in time. It's important to know when that moment is and remember it forever.

It's completely normal to feel nervous at this stage. If you have a few butterflies in your stomach, that's fine; it's no threat to your chances of success. Rather like making a parachute jump, your nervousness will quickly turn to exhilaration as you jump and realize that everything you've learned and prepared for is working exactly how you've been told it would. The feeling is one of incredible freedom and elation.

You are in that position now, standing by the plane door, ready to jump. You have all the knowledge and understanding you need to make this the best experience of your life. The nerves are perfectly natural and normal. Soon you will be flying free.

You have nothing to fear. Unlike parachuting, there is no risk whatsoever. No risk but the greatest reward. All that's left to do is to cement the moment in your mind when you commit to becoming a happy, healthy eater for life.

Remind yourself that you are not "giving up" anything. If you've followed and understood everything, you'll come to the obvious conclusion:

THERE IS NO PLEASURE OR COMFORT IN EATING JUNK FOOD

IN HER OWN WORDS: PAULINE

It's an incredible moment when you realize you have unraveled the brainwashing and freed yourself from the slavery of emotional eating. It's like a door has been opened; illusions have been swept out and the truth has rushed in. The brilliant thing about Easyway is that whatever skepticism you might feel at the beginning gives way to realization, just by following the instructions.

I despised myself, but at the same time I felt the constant need to be comforted. So I was punishing myself and rewarding myself at the same time, and I was using the same thing for both: Junk food. Looking back, I find it incredible that I couldn't see the obvious truth: That it was the food that was making me feel this way, but that's what addiction does to you.

Easyway freed me from that and made me feel happier, healthier, and more in control than I could ever imagine. The amazing thing was that I didn't have to make a conscious decision to eat more healthily, my appetite for junk just disappeared and my enjoyment of more nutritious food soared. Simple as that!

Very soon I will ask you to make a solemn vow that you will never again seek comfort or pleasure from junk food. Before you do, it's essential that you are completely clear that junk food gives you no pleasure or comfort whatsoever and, therefore, you are not making any sort of sacrifice.

You are now going to prove that point to yourself. I want you to choose something for your Final Feast, something that you recently regarded as your favorite snack. A chocolate bar, a cake, a bag of potato chips or box of cookies, donuts, or whatever... the choice is yours.

Hold the food and look at it carefully. Think about the misery that your desire for this and other types of junk food has caused you and how helpless you felt when you were in the trap—wanting to quit but feeling powerless to do so. Think about the hours you've wasted and the money you've squandered. Most of all, think about the constant lack of satisfaction that has kept you chasing an impossible goal.

Now think about everything you are about to gain by quitting. More time, more money, better health, higher self-esteem, more control, more freedom. Think how good it will feel not to be able to eat every meal without despising yourself for your lack of discipline. Think of the relief of being able to live your life free from deceit and guilt. Think how good it will feel not to be a slave.

As you look at the food in your hand, ask yourself how it looks and smells. Is there any aroma? What does it remind you of? How is this piece of processed emptiness making you feel? Are you excited to eat it? Or does it look a bit bland?

OK, take a bite and pay attention to your senses of taste and feel. How would you describe the flavor? What happens to the consistency of the food as you hold it in your mouth? Is that a good feeling? OK, now swallow that mouthful and go through the process again. Keep going until the food is all finished. If you find that hard, be aware of the actual feeling of not wanting to eat any more and remind yourself of everything you know and understand about the food in your hand:

- It gives you no genuine pleasure or comfort.

- It doesn't relieve stress, anxiety, or loneliness; it causes them.

- The only reason you ever thought it did was because you were brainwashed.

Now take a deep breath and make a solemn vow that you will never eat junk food for comfort or pleasure again. **EVER!** Be certain about the decision you're making, embrace the moment, and greet it with a sense of triumph. "Yes! I'm no longer an emotional eater. I'm FREE!"

DON'T WAIT FOR THE OUTCOME

You're free from the moment you complete your Final Feast and make your vow. The ritual marks the start of your new life, breaking of the cycle of addiction. And that's it. There is nothing to wait for. You're now a happy, healthy eater. Congratulations!

Enjoy your victory. This is one of the greatest achievements of your life, if not the greatest. It's important that this moment is firmly implanted in your mind. Right now you are fired up with powerful reasons to stop, but be aware that in a few days your resolution will fade and you'll relax into a normal life. As the days, weeks, and years go by, your memory of how miserable emotional eating once made you feel will dim.

So fix those thoughts in your mind now while they are vivid, so that even if your memory of the details should diminish, your resolution never to eat junk for pleasure or comfort does not.

Chapter 19

ENJOYING LIFE FREE FROM EMOTIONAL EATING

IN THIS CHAPTER

• *THE FIRST FEW DAYS* • *ALL YOU HAVE GAINED*
• *WHEN THINGS GO WRONG* • *START LIVING NOW*

Congratulations! You are now ready to get on and enjoy the marvelous pleasures of life free from emotional eating. Just make sure you remain aware that there will be moments when you need to remind yourself of everything you have learned.

For a few days after your Final Feast, you may still feel the Little Monster crying as it goes through its death throes. There is no need to fear this feeling, but you shouldn't try to ignore it either. Now that you're aware of what it is, you can congratulate yourself on taking control and enjoy feeling the Little Monster die.

This is the withdrawal period that is made out to be such an ordeal, especially by people who have tried to quit with the willpower method. For them it often is an ordeal, because they respond to the Little Monster's death throes by thinking, "I'd like a snack." This triggers a mental struggle, which causes the physical symptoms associated with withdrawal.

Without that mental struggle, the withdrawal period is no problem. Living with the death throes is no harder than living with a slight bout of flu and they only last for a few days. In fact you'll barely notice them. They only become a problem if you start to worry about them or interpret them as a need or desire to eat junk. If you do feel them, picture a Little Monster searching around the desert for food and you having control of the supply. All you have to do is keep the supply line closed. It's as easy as that.

Instead of thinking, "I fancy a snack but I'm not allowed to," think, "YIPPEE! I'm FREE! This is what emotional eaters suffer throughout their addicted lives. Happy, healthy eaters don't have to suffer this feeling. Isn't it great! I'm a happy healthy, eater." Think this way and those withdrawal pangs will become moments of pleasure.

Remember to pay attention to your senses. Focus on the feeling and allow yourself to become aware that there is no physical pain—the only discomfort you might be feeling is not because you've stopped eating junk but because you started in the first place. Also be clear that if you were to try to stop the feeling by eating junk again, far from relieving that discomfort, you would insure that you suffered it for the rest of your life.

Take pleasure in starving that Little Monster. Revel in its death throes. Feel no guilt about rejoicing in its death.

WHEN THINGS GO WRONG

Of course, there will be days when you find it hard to see the joy in life. That's perfectly normal. Everybody has days when everything that can go wrong does go wrong. It has nothing to do with the fact that you've stopped eating junk food. In fact, when you stop eating junk, you find that the bad days don't come around so frequently.

For people who quit with the willpower method, bad days can be the trigger that leads them back to emotional eating. Because they don't understand about the brainwashing, even long after the physical withdrawal has ended, they will interpret normal feelings of stress or irritability or even hunger as a need or desire to eat junk. They won't want to, though, because they have made a huge effort to quit, so they will feel deprived and that will make the stress and irritability worse.

Sooner or later their willpower will give out and they will "treat themselves." They'll tell themselves it's "just the once," but very soon they will find themselves hooked again. If their willpower doesn't give out, they will spend the rest of their lives enduring the agony of wondering when the sense of deprivation will end.

You might well find that when you have bad days, the thought of eating junk food enters your mind. Don't worry about it, and don't try to push it to one side either. Remember the elephants! You cannot tell your brain to *not* think about something. If you try to *not* think about eating junk food, you will get frustrated and miserable.

But that doesn't mean you're putting yourself at risk. When you have no desire to eat junk food, you can think about it all you like. What's more, you can remind yourself of the marvelous truth. Whereas someone who tries to quit with willpower will think, "I mustn't eat junk," or, "I thought I'd beaten this craving," you'll be thinking, "Great! I'm a happy, healthy eater! I'm free!"

My fourth instruction was never to doubt or question your decision to quit. This is essential. If you allow doubt to creep in, you will allow the Big Monster back in and soon you'll be back in the trap.

Prepare yourself for the bad days and have your mindset ready. Protect yourself against getting caught out by them. Be ready for feelings of stress, irritability, sadness, loneliness, disappointment, or apathy and remind yourself that you are better equipped to handle them now than you were as an emotional eater. Eating junk would only make them worse.

Be absolutely clear that there is no such thing as "just the once." If the thought of having "just one binge" ever enters your mind, replace it with the thought, "Yippee! I'm a happy, healthy eater! I have set myself free from that life of misery." The thought will pass very quickly and your brain will accept that there is no future in thinking that way.

START LIVING NOW

The wonderful thing about overcoming emotional eating with Easyway is not just that it takes away the struggle but that you don't have to wait for the Little Monster to die before you start enjoying life again. Freedom begins the moment you finish your Final Feast and make your vow.

IT'S TIME TO GET ON WITH LIFE

On the one hand, you're freeing yourself from slavery; on the other, you're about to rediscover life's genuine pleasures. It's a win-win.

Emotional eating, like all addictions, takes away the ability to enjoy the things that you used to enjoy: reading books, watching entertainment, social occasions, exercise, making love... Because you regard your little fix as the only thing that can relieve your craving, nothing else gives you satisfaction. Now that you are a happy, healthy eater, you have all these pleasures to get excited about again.

You will find that situations you had come to regard as unstimulating or even irritating become enjoyable again: Things like spending time with your loved ones, going for walks, seeing friends. Work too will become more enjoyable, as you find you are better able to concentrate, to think creatively, and to handle stress. Life becomes so much easier when you're not being dragged all over the place, physically and mentally, by emotional eating.

Most importantly, you will rediscover the pleasure of meal times. Instead of being a source of guilt and self-loathing, the food you eat will be a genuine pleasure, leaving you feeling satisfied, energetic, and happy. Enjoy eating when you feel like it, rather than when the monsters drive you to it. Enjoy the flavor and variety of nutritious foods. Enjoy not suffering the bloated feeling or sluggishness caused by indigestible junk food; or the feeling of gluttony after bingeing uncontrollably on junk.

Remember, you were designed to enjoy eating. Now you can get on and do it.

YOU ARE FREE!

Chapter 20

USEFUL REMINDERS

From time to time, you may find it useful to remind yourself of some of the issues that we've discussed. Here I have summarized the key points, together with a reminder of the instructions. Follow these and you will remain a happy, healthy eater for the rest of your life.

If you have turned straight to this page, hoping to find a short-cut to the solution to your emotional eating problem, I'm afraid that won't work. You need to start from the beginning and read all the way through the book in order. Once you've done that, the following reminders will make perfect sense.

- Don't wait for anything. You are free from the moment you unravel the brainwashing and kill the Big Monster and you can get on with life as a happy, healthy eater as soon as you complete the ritual of the Final Feast. You've cut off the supply to the Little Monster and unlocked the door of your prison.

- Accept that there will always be good days and bad days, but remember that you will be stronger both physically and mentally, and so you'll enjoy the good times and handle the bad times better.

- Be aware that a very important change is happening in your life. Like all major changes, including those for the better, it can take time for your mind and body to adjust. Don't worry if you feel different or disoriented for a few days. It's all part of the wonderful achievement of getting free.

- Remember you've stopped bingeing on junk food, you haven't stopped living. You can now start enjoying life to the full.

- There is no need to avoid other emotional eaters. Go out and enjoy social occasions and show yourself you can handle situations without feeling tempted to eat junk right from the start.

- Don't envy junk food addicts. When you're with them, remember you're not being deprived, they are. They will be envying you because they will be wishing they could be like you: **FREE**.

- Forget using substitutes to help you through the withdrawal period. You will just be perpetuating the myth that quitting is hard. You don't need any sort of substitute and they don't work anyway.

- Never doubt or question your decision to stop—you know it's the right one. If the thought enters your head that life will be less enjoyable without your junk food addiction, just remember how miserable it felt to be in the grip of the Big Monster. If you allow temptation to creep in, you will put yourself in an impossible position: Miserable if you don't and even more miserable if you do.

- Make sure right from the start that if the thought of "just one binge" enters your mind, you respond with the thought, "YIPPEE! I no longer have any desire to do that. I'm a happy, healthy eater." The thought will pass very quickly and your brain will quickly learn not to think it again.

- Don't try *not* to think about eating junk, it doesn't work. It's impossible to make your brain not think about something. By trying to you will make yourself frustrated and miserable. It's easy to think about junk food without feeling miserable: instead of thinking, "I mustn't eat it," or, "When will the craving stop?" think, "Great! I'm a happy, healthy eater. It's fantastic that I'm free!"

- If you want to, share your achievement with those who are close to you. Come clean with everyone who has been affected by your emotional eating and let them join in your elation at getting free. If you feel the need to reach out for help, guidance, or advice then please do contact us via www. allencarr.com. We're always happy to hear from book readers, especially if they need just a little extra advice. There is also a great Facebook group for people breaking free from Bad Sugar addiction, so feel free to check that out too. Search on Facebook for "Allen Carr's GOOD SUGAR BAD SUGAR" group.

THE INSTRUCTIONS

1 FOLLOW ALL THE INSTRUCTIONS

2 OPEN YOUR MIND

3 BEGIN WITH A FEELING OF ELATION

4 NEVER DOUBT YOUR DECISION TO QUIT

5 IGNORE ALL ADVICE AND INFLUENCES THAT CONFLICT WITH EASYWAY

6 AVOID EATING, UNLESS YOU ARE HUNGRY

7 NEVER AGAIN EAT FOOD FOR COMFORT

8 DON'T WAIT FOR THE RIGHT TIME TO QUIT; DO IT NOW!

YIPPEE!
I'M FREE

ALLEN CARR'S EASYWAY CENTERS

The following list indicates the countries where Allen Carr's Easyway To Stop Smoking Centers are currently operational.

Check www.allencarr.com for latest additions to this list.

The success rate at the centers, based on the three-month money-back guarantee, is over 90 percent.

Selected centers also offer sessions that deal with alcohol, other drugs, and weight issues. Please check with your nearest center, listed over the page, for details.

Allen Carr's Easyway guarantees that you will find it easy to stop at the centres or your money back.

JOIN US!

Allen Carr's Easyway Centers have spread throughout the world with incredible speed and success. Our global franchise network now covers more than 150 cities in 50 countries worldwide. This amazing growth has been achieved entirely organically. Former addicts, just like you, were so impressed by the ease with which they stopped that they felt inspired to contact us to see how they could bring the method to their region.

If you feel the same, contact us for details on how to become an Allen Carr's Easyway To Stop Smoking or an Allen Carr's Easyway To Stop Drinking franchisee.

Email us at: join-us@allencarr.com including your full name, postal address, and region of interest.

SUPPORT US!

No, don't send us money!

You have achieved something really marvelous. Every time we hear of someone escaping from the sinking ship, we get a feeling of enormous satisfaction.

It would give us great pleasure to hear that you have freed yourself from the slavery of addiction, so please visit the following web page where you can tell us of your success, inspire others to follow in your footsteps, and hear about ways you can help to spread the word.

www.allencarr.com/fanzone

You can "like" our Facebook page here **www.facebook.com/AllenCarr**

Together, we can help further Allen Carr's mission: to cure the world of addiction.

ALLEN CARR'S EASYWAY CENTERS

WORLDWIDE HEAD OFFICE
Allen Carr's Easyway
Park House, 14 Pepys Road,
Raynes Park, London SW20 8NH
ENGLAND
Tel: +44 (0)208 9447761
Email: mail@allencarr.com
Website: www.allencarr.com

WORLDWIDE PRESS OFFICE
Tel: +44 (0)7970 88 44 52
Contact: John Dicey
Email: media@allencarr.com

NORTH AMERICAN CENTERS

U.S.A.
Sessions held throughout the USA
Toll free: 855 440 3777
Email: receptionteam@allencarr.com
Website: www.allencarr.com

New York
Toll free: 855 440 3777
Therapists: Natalie Clays and Team
Email: receptionteam@allencarr.com
Website: www.allencarr.com

Los Angeles
Toll free: 855 440 3777
Therapists: Natalie Clays and Team
Email: receptionteam@allencarr.com
Website: www.allencarr.com

**Milwaukee
(and South Wisconsin)**
Tel: +1 262 770 1260
Therapist: Wayne Spaulding
Email:
wayne@easywaywisconsin.com
Website: www.allencarr.com

CANADA
Sessions held throughout Canada
Email: receptionteam@allencarr.com
Website: www.allencarr.com

U.K. CENTERS

Birmingham
Tel & Fax: 0800 389 2115
Therapists: John Dicey, Colleen
Dwyer, Crispin Hay, Emma
Hudson, Rob Fielding, Sam Kelser,
Rob Groves, Debbie Brewer-West,
Gerry Williams (alcohol)
Email: mail@allencarr.com
Website: www.allencarr.com

Bournemouth
Tel: 0800 389 2115
Therapists: John Dicey, Colleen
Dwyer, Crispin Hay, Emma
Hudson, Rob Fielding, Sam Kelser,
Rob Groves, Debbie Brewer-West
Email: mail@allencarr.com
Website: www.allencarr.com

Brentwood
Tel: 0800 389 2115
Therapists: John Dicey, Colleen
Dwyer, Crispin Hay, Emma
Hudson, Rob Fielding, Sam Kelser,
Rob Groves, Debbie Brewer-West
Email: mail@allencarr.com
Website: www.allencarr.com

Brighton
Tel: 0800 389 2115
Therapists: John Dicey, Colleen
Dwyer, Crispin Hay, Emma
Hudson, Rob Fielding, Sam Kelser,
Rob Groves, Debbie Brewer-West
Email: mail@allencarr.com
Website: www.allencarr.com

Bristol
Tel: 0800 389 2115
Therapists: John Dicey, Colleen
Dwyer, Crispin Hay, Emma
Hudson, Rob Fielding, Sam Kelser,
Rob Groves, Debbie Brewer-West
Email: mail@allencarr.com
Website: www.allencarr.com

Cambridge
Tel: 0800 389 2115
Therapists: John Dicey, Colleen
Dwyer, Crispin Hay, Emma
Hudson, Rob Fielding, Sam Kelser,
Rob Groves, Debbie Brewer-West
Email: mail@allencarr.com
Website: www.allencarr.com

Coventry
Tel: 0800 321 3007
Therapist: Rob Fielding
Email:
info@easywaymidlands.co.uk
Website: www.allencarr.com

Cumbria
Tel: 0800 077 6187
Therapist: Mark Keen
Email:
mark@easywaymanchester.co.uk
Website: www.allencarr.com

Derby
Tel: 0800 389 2115
Therapists: John Dicey, Colleen
Dwyer, Crispin Hay, Emma
Hudson, Rob Fielding, Sam Kelser,
Rob Groves, Debbie Brewer-West
Email: mail@allencarr.com
Website: www.allencarr.com

Guernsey

Tel: 0800 077 6187
Therapist: Mark Keen
Email:
mark@easywaymanchester.co.uk
Website: www.allencarr.com

Isle of Man

Tel: 0800 077 6187
Therapist: Mark Keen
Email: mark@easywaymanchester.
co.uk
Website: www.allencarr.com

Jersey

Tel: 0800 077 6187
Therapist: Mark Keen
Email:
mark@easywaymanchester.co.uk
Website: www.allencarr.com

Kent

Tel: 0800 389 2115
Therapists: John Dicey, Colleen
Dwyer, Crispin Hay, Emma
Hudson, Rob Fielding, Sam Kelser,
Rob Groves, Debbie Brewer-West
Email: mail@allencarr.com
Website: www.allencarr.com

Lancashire

Tel: 0800 077 6187
Therapist: Mark Keen
Email:
mark@easywaymanchester.co.uk
Website: www.allencarr.com

Leeds

Tel: 0800 077 6187
Therapist: Mark Keen
Email:
mark@easywaymanchester.co.uk
Website: www.allencarr.com

Leicester

Tel: 0800 321 3007
Therapist: Rob Fielding
Email:
info@easywaymidlands.co.uk
Website: www.allencarr.com

Lincoln

Tel: 0800 321 3007
Therapist: Rob Fielding
Email:
info@easywaymidlands.co.uk
Website: www.allencarr.com

Liverpool

Tel: 0800 077 6187
Therapist: Mark Keen
Email:
mark@easywaymanchester.co.uk
Website: www.allencarr.com

London

Tel: 020 8944 7761
Therapists: John Dicey, Colleen
Dwyer, Crispin Hay, Emma
Hudson, Rob Fielding, Sam Kelser,
Rob Groves, Debbie Brewer-West,
Duncan Bhaskaran-Brown, Gerry
Williams (Alcohol), Monique
Douglas (Weight)
Email: mail@allencarr.com
Website: www.allencarr.com

Manchester

Tel: 0800 077 6187

Therapist: Mark Keen

Email:
mark@easywaymanchester.co.uk

Website: www.allencarr.com

Manchester—alcohol sessions

Tel: +44 (0)7936 712942

Therapist: Mike Connolly

Email:
info@stopdrinkingnorth.co.uk

Website: www.allencarr.com

Milton Keynes

Tel: 0800 389 2115

Therapists: John Dicey, Colleen
Dwyer, Crispin Hay, Emma
Hudson, Rob Fielding, Sam Kelser,
Rob Groves, Debbie Brewer-West

Email: mail@allencarr.com

Website: www.allencarr.com

Newcastle/North East

Tel: 0800 077 6187

Therapist: Mark Keen

Email:
mark@easywaymanchester.co.uk

Website: www.allencarr.com

Northern Ireland/Belfast

Tel: 0800 077 6187

Therapist: Mark Keen

Email:
mark@easywaymanchester.co.uk

Website: www.allencarr.com

Nottingham

Tel: 0800 389 2115

Therapists: John Dicey, Colleen
Dwyer, Crispin Hay, Emma
Hudson, Rob Fielding, Sam Kelser,
Rob Groves, Debbie Brewer-West

Email: mail@allencarr.com

Website: www.allencarr.com

Oxford

Tel: 0800 389 2115

Therapists: John Dicey, Colleen
Dwyer, Crispin Hay, Emma
Hudson, Rob Fielding, Sam Kelser,
Rob Groves, Debbie Brewer-West

Email: mail@allencarr.com

Website: www.allencarr.com

Reading

Tel: 0800 389 2115

Therapists: John Dicey, Colleen
Dwyer, Crispin Hay, Emma
Hudson, Rob Fielding, Sam Kelser,
Rob Groves, Debbie Brewer-West

Email: mail@allencarr.com

Website: www.allencarr.com

SCOTLAND
Glasgow and Edinburgh

Tel: +44 (0)131 449 7858

Therapists: Paul Melvin and Jim
McCreadie

Email: info@easywayscotland.co.uk

Website: www.allencarr.com

Southampton

Tel: 0800 389 2115
Therapists: John Dicey, Colleen
Dwyer, Crispin Hay, Emma
Hudson, Rob Fielding, Sam Kelser,
Rob Groves, Debbie Brewer-West
Email: mail@allencarr.com
Website: www.allencarr.com

Southport

Tel: 0800 077 6187
Therapist: Mark Keen
Email:
mark@easywaymanchester.co.uk
Website: www.allencarr.com

Staines/Heathrow

Tel: 0800 389 2115
Therapists: John Dicey, Colleen
Dwyer, Crispin Hay, Emma
Hudson, Rob Fielding, Sam Kelser,
Rob Groves, Debbie Brewer-West
Email: mail@allencarr.com
Website: www.allencarr.com

Stevenage

Tel: 0800 389 2115
Therapists: John Dicey, Colleen
Dwyer, Crispin Hay, Emma
Hudson, Rob Fielding, Sam Kelser,
Rob Groves, Debbie Brewer-West
Email: mail@allencarr.com
Website: www.allencarr.com

Stoke

Tel: 0800 389 2115
Therapists: John Dicey, Colleen
Dwyer, Crispin Hay, Emma
Hudson, Rob Fielding, Sam Kelser,
Rob Groves, Debbie Brewer-West
Email: mail@allencarr.com
Website: www.allencarr.com

Surrey

Park House, 14 Pepys Road, Raynes
Park, London SW20 8NH
Tel: +44 (0)20 8944 7761
Fax: +44 (0)20 8944 8619
Therapists: John Dicey, Colleen
Dwyer, Crispin Hay, Emma
Hudson, Rob Fielding, Sam Kelser,
Rob Groves, Debbie Brewer-West,
Duncan Bhaskaran-Brown, Gerry
Williams (Alcohol), Monique
Douglas (Weight)
Email: mail@allencarr.com
Website: www.allencarr.com

Watford

Tel: 0800 389 2115
Therapists: John Dicey, Colleen
Dwyer, Crispin Hay, Emma
Hudson, Rob Fielding, Sam Kelser,
Rob Groves, Debbie Brewer-West
Email: mail@allencarr.com
Website: www.allencarr.com

Worcester

Tel: 0800 321 3007
Therapist: Rob Fielding
Email:
info@easywaymidlands.co.uk
Website: www.allencarr.com

WORLDWIDE CENTERS

AUSTRALIA
ACT, NSW, NT, QLD, VIC
Tel: 1300 848 028
Therapist: Natalie Clays and Team
Email: natalie@allencarr.com.au
Website: www.allencarr.com

South Australia
Tel: 1300 848 028
Therapist: Jaime Reed
Email: sa@allencarr.com.au
Website: www.allencarr.com

Western Australia
Tel: 1300 848 028
Therapist: Natalie Clays and Team
Email: natalie@allencarr.com.au
Website: www.allencarr.com

AUSTRIA
Sessions held throughout Austria
Freephone: 0800RAUCHEN
(0800 7282436)
Tel: +43 (0)3512 44755
Therapists: Erich Kellermann and Team
Email: info@allen-carr.at
Website: www.allencarr.com

BAHRAIN
Tel: 00966501306090
Website: www.allencarr.com

BELGIUM
Antwerp
Tel: +32 (0)3 281 6255
Fax: +32 (0)3 744 0608
Therapist: Dirk Nielandt
Email: info@allencarr.be
Website: www.allencarr.com

BRAZIL
Therapist: Lilian Brunstein
Email: lilian@easywaysp.com.br
Website: www.allencarr.com

BULGARIA
Tel: 0800 14104 / +359 899 88 99 07
Therapist: Rumyana Kostadinova
Email: rk@nepushaveche.com
Website: www.allencarr.com

CHILE
Tel: +56 2 4744587
Therapist: Claudia Sarmiento
Email: contacto@allencarr.cl
Website: www.allencarr.com

CYPRUS
Please check website for details
Email: mail@allencarr.com
Website: www.allencarr.com

DENMARK
Sessions held throughout Denmark
Tel: +45 70267711
Therapist: Mette Fønss
Email: mette@easyway.dk
Website: www.allencarr.com

ESTONIA

Tel: +372 733 0044
Therapist: Henry Jakobson
Email: info@allencarr.ee
Website: www.allencarr.com

FINLAND

Tel: +358-(0)45 3544099
Therapist: Janne Ström
Email: info@allencarr.fi
Website: www.allencarr.com

FRANCE

Sessions held throughout France
Freephone: 0800 386387
Tel: +33 (4)91 33 54 55
Therapists: Erick Serre and Team
Email: info@allencarr.fr
Website: www.allencarr.com

GERMANY

Sessions held throughout Germany
Freephone: 08000RAUCHEN
(0800 07282436)
Tel: +49 (0) 8031 90190-0
Therapists: Erich Kellermann
and Team
Email: info@allen-carr.de
Website: www.allencarr.com

GREECE

Sessions held throughout Greece
Tel: +30 210 5224087
Therapist: Panos Tzouras
Email: panos@allencarr.gr
Website: www.allencarr.com

GUATEMALA

Tel: +502 2362 0000

Therapist: Michelle Binford
Email:
info@dejadefumarfacil.com
Website: www.allencarr.com

HONG KONG

Email: info@easywayhongkong.com
Website: www.allencarr.com

HUNGARY

Seminars in Budapest and
12 other cities across Hungary
Tel: 06 80 624 426 (freephone) or
+36 20 580 9244
Therapist: Gábor Szász
Email: szasz.gabor@allencarr.hu
Website: www.allencarr.com

INDIA
Bangalore and Chennai

Tel: +91 (0)80 4154 0624
Therapist: Suresh Shottam
Email: info@
easywaytostopsmoking.co.in
Website: www.allencarr.com

IRAN
Tehran and Mashhad

Please check website for details
Website: www.allencarr.com

ISRAEL

Sessions held throughout Israel
Tel: +972 (0)3 6212525
Therapists: Ramy Romanovsky,
Orit Rozen
Email: info@allencarr.co.il
Website: www.allencarr.com

ITALY

Sessions held throughout Italy

Tel/Fax: +39 (0)2 7060 2438
Therapists: Francesca Cesati and Team
Email: info@easywayitalia.com
Website: www.allencarr.com

JAPAN

Sessions held throughout Japan
www.allencarr.com

LEBANON

Tel: +961 1 791 5565
Therapist: Sadek El-Assaad
Email: info@AllenCarrEasyWay.me
Website: www.allencarr.com

MAURITIUS

Tel: +230 5727 5103
Therapist: Heidi Hoareau
Email: info@allencarr.mu
Website: www.allencarr.com

MEXICO

Sessions held throughout Mexico
Tel: +52 55 2623 0631
Therapists: Jorge Davo and Team
Email: info@allencarr-mexico.com
Website: www.allencarr.com

NETHERLANDS

Sessions held throughout the
Netherlands
Allen Carr's Easyway
'stoppen met roken'
Tel: (+31)53 478 43 62 /
(+31)900 786 77 37
Email: info@allencarr.nl
Website: www.allencarr.com

NEW ZEALAND
North Island – Auckland

Tel: +64 (0) 800 848 028

Therapist: Natalie Clays and Team
Email: natalie@allencarr.co.nz
Website: www.allencarr.com

South Island – Wellington and Christchurch

Tel: +64 (0) 800 848 028
Therapist: Natalie Clays and Team
Email: natalie@allencarr.co.nz
Website: www.allencarr.com

South Island – Dunedin and Invercargill

Tel: +64 (0)27 4139 381
Therapist: Debbie Kinder
Email: easywaysouth@icloud.com
Website: www.allencarr.com

NORWAY

Therapist: Laila Thorsen
Please check website for details
Website: www.allencarr.com

PERU
Lima

Tel: +511 637 7310
Therapist: Luis Loranca
Email: lloranca@
dejardefumaraltoque.com
Website: www.allencarr.com

POLAND

Sessions held throughout Poland
Tel: +48 (0)22 621 36 11
Therapist: Michael Kochon
Email: info@allen-carr.pl
Website: www.allencarr.com

PORTUGAL
Oporto

Tel: +351 22 9958698

Therapist: Ria Slof
Email:
info@comodeixardefumar.com
Website: www.allencarr.com

REPUBLIC OF IRELAND
Dublin
Tel: +353 (0)1 499 9010
Therapists: Paul Melvin & Jim
McCreadie
Email: info@allencarr.ie
Website: www.allencarr.com

ROMANIA
Tel: +40 (0)7321 3 8383
Therapist: Cristina Nichita
Email: raspunsuri@allencarr.ro
Website: www.allencarr.com

RUSSIA
Tel: +7 495 644 64 26
Freecall +7 (800) 250 6622
Therapist: Alexander Fomin
Email: info@allencarr.ru
Website: www.allencarr.com

Allen Carr's Easyway to Stop
Drinking Live Seminars & Online
Video Program
Tel: +8 (800) 302 80 68
+7 985 207 47 93
Therapist: Artem Kasyanov
Email: info@allencarrlife.ru
Website: www.allencarr.com

St Petersburg
Please check website for details
Website: www.allencarr.com

SAUDI ARABIA
Tel: 00966501306090
Website: www.allencarr.com

SERBIA
Belgrade
Tel: +381 (0)11 308 8686
Email: office@allencarr.co.rs
Website: www.allencarr.com

SINGAPORE
Tel: +65 62241450
Therapist: Pam Oei
Email: pam@allencarr.com.sg
Website: www.allencarr.com

SLOVENIA
Tel: 00386 (0)40 77 61 77
Therapist: Grega Sever
Email: easyway@easyway.si
Website: www.allencarr.com

SOUTH AFRICA
Sessions held throughout South
Africa
National Booking Line:
0861 100 200
Head Office: 15 Draper Square,
Draper St, Claremont 7708, Cape
Town, Cape Town
Tel: +27 (0)21 851 5883
Mobile: 083 600 5555
Therapists: Dr Charles Nel,
Malcolm Robinson and Team
Email: easyway@allencarr.co.za
Website: www.allencarr.com

SOUTH KOREA
Seoul
Tel: +82 (0)70 4227 1862

Therapist: Yousung Cha

Email: master@allencarr.co.kr

Website: www.allencarr.com

SPAIN

Tel: +34 910 05 29 99

Therapists: Luis Loranca

Email: informes@AllenCarrOfficial.es

Website: www.allencarr.com

SWEDEN

Tel: +46 70 695 6850

Therapists: Nina Ljungqvist,

Renée Johansson

Email: info@easyway.se

Website: www.allencarr.com

SWITZERLAND

Sessions held throughout

Switzerland

Freephone: 0800RAUCHEN

(0800/728 2436)

Tel: +41 (0)52 383 3773

Fax: +41 (0)52 3833774

Therapists: Cyrill Argast and Team

For sessions in Suisse Romand

and Svizzera Italiana:

Tel: 0800 386 387

Email: info@allen-carr.ch

Website: www.allencarr.com

TURKEY

Sessions held throughout Turkey

Tel: +90 212 358 5307

Therapist: Emre Üstünuçar

Email: info@allencarrturkiye.com

Website: www.allencarr.com

UNITED ARAB EMIRATES
Dubai and Abu Dhabi

Tel: +971 56 693 4000

Therapist: Sadek El-Assaad

Email: info@AllenCarrEasyWay.me

Website: www.allencarr.com

OTHER ALLEN CARR PUBLICATIONS

Allen Carr's revolutionary Easyway method is available in a wide variety of formats, including digitally as audiobooks and ebooks, and has been successfully applied to a broad range of subjects. For more information about Easyway publications, please visit

shop.allencarr.com

Good Sugar Bad Sugar

The Easy Way to Quit Sugar

The Easy Way to Lose Weight

Allen Carr's Easy Way for Women to Lose Weight

No More Diets

Allen Carr's Easy Way to Quit Smoking Without Willpower

The Illustrated Easy Way to Stop Smoking

Allen Carr's Easy Way for Women to Quit Smoking

The Illustrated Easy Way for Women to Stop Smoking

Your Personal Stop Smoking Plan

Smoking Sucks (Parent Guide with 16 page pull-out comic)

Finally Free!

The Little Book of Quitting Smoking

How to Be a Happy Nonsmoker

No More Ashtrays

The Only Way to Stop Smoking Permanently

How to Stop Your Child Smoking

The Easy Way to Control Alcohol

Allen Carr's Quit Drinking Without Willpower

Your Personal Stop Drinking Plan

Allen Carr's Easy Way for Women to Quit Drinking

The Illustrated Easy Way to Stop Drinking

No More Hangovers

The Easy Way to Mindfulness

Smart Phone Dumb Phone

The Easy Way to Stop Gambling

No More Gambling

No More Worrying

Get Out of Debt Now

No More Debt

No More Fear of Flying

The Easy Way to Quit Caffeine

Packing It In The Easy Way
(the autobiography)

Want Easyway on your **smartphone** or **tablet**?
Search for "Allen Carr" in your app store.

Easyway publications are also available as **audiobooks**.
Visit **shop.allencarr.com** to find out more.

DISCOUNT VOUCHER
for
ALLEN CARR'S
EASYWAY CENTERS

Recover the price of this book when you attend an
Allen Carr's Easyway Center
anywhere in the world!

Allen Carr's Easyway has a global network of stop
smoking centers where we guarantee you'll find it easy
to stop smoking or your money back.

**The success rate based on this
unique money-back guarantee is over 90%.**

Sessions addressing weight, alcohol and other
drug addictions are also available at certain centers.

When you book your session, mention this
voucher and you'll receive a discount of
the price of this book. Contact your nearest
center for more information on how the sessions
work and to book your appointment.

**Details of Allen Carr's Easyway
Centers can be found at**
www.allencarr.com